# PITCH OF LIFE

## Writings on Cricket

## Chris Searle

WITH A FOREWORD BY MIKE MARQUSEE

## The Parrs Wood Press
## MANCHESTER

First Published 2001

**THE PARRS WOOD PRESS**
St Wilfrid's Enterprise Centre
Royce Road, Manchester, M15 5BJ
www.parrswoodpress.com


© Chris Searle 2001


**ISBN: 1 903158 19 2**


This book was produced by Andrew Searle and Helen Faulkner of The Parrs Wood Press and Printed in Great Britain by:


Fretwell Print & Design
Healey Works
Goulbourne Street
Keighley
West Yorkshire
BD21 1PZ

# CONTENTS

# ACKNOWLEDGEMENTS

To the memory of my father, Dick Searle (1908-1993), cricketer of Essex: and to my mother Winifred (1913-1993), who washed his dirty whites for three-and-a-half decades; Pearl and our sons Victor, Kevin, Daniel and Russell who knock over different stumps; and the young cricketers of Fir Vale, Sheffield who hold the bat and ball of the future with their team-mates all over the world.

I thank too my dear friends at the Institute of Race Relations, London, and the critical and editorial suggestions of the editors of its international journal, *Race and Class*, A. Sivanandan and Hazel Waters. My chapters 'Race Before Wicket', 'Cricket and the Mirror of Racism', 'Lara's Innings' and 'Towards a Cricket of the Future' were first published as articles in the journal.

'The Echoing Street' was first published in the journal of Hit Racism for Six, and the articles on Amir Riaz, Devon Malcolm and 'Racism on the Western Terrace' were first published in the *Observer*. Many of the reviews included in the 'Cricket in Print' chapter first saw light of day in the *Morning Star*, as did the article on Courtney Walsh and Curtly Ambrose. 'Pitch of Life: Re-reading CLR James' Beyond a Boundary' was first published in *Race, Sport and British Society*, edited by Ben Carrington and Ian McDonald and published by Routledge in 2001. My gratitude to Kevin Mitchell for his permission to reproduce his *Observer* article, 'Mean Streets feel the pace of change', as an appendix. Finally, my thanks too to dear cricketing friend Mike Marqusee for his words of introduction, to Andrew Searle and Helen Faulkner of the Parrs Wood Press and to Patricia Hardwicke for her painstaking word processing.

# FOREWORD

It was through reading Chris Searle's articles on cricket in *Race and Class* that I realised I was not alone. When Chris wrote about the English cricket establishment's love affair with apartheid, or the struggles of young Caribbean and Asian cricketers forging their way in Britain's inner cities, or the genius of West Indies' batsmen and bowlers, I recognised in print the real contours of the game I myself had grown to know and relish (unlike Chris) only as an adult.

Reading Chris Searle on cricket was liberating. Yes, it was possible to love cricket from the left. More than that, it was impossible to understand the game - and therefore to love it to the full - without placing it in the wider context of contending social forces. And, of course, Chris didn't see this connection as a detached neutral. His writing on cricket was part and parcel of his intellectual, social and political commitment.

In the spirit of his revered master, C.L.R. James, Searle is not afraid to blend autobiography with historical analysis, and by following the strands of his own life - as cricketer, teacher, spectator - he is able to explore the interwoven textures of the global game. For him, cricket isn't about scores and averages, and technique is of interest mainly as a window on to the soul of the player. In these articles, the reader will find a human drama far more compelling than the gossip and waffle that fill so much of today's sports pages. It is the drama of how a game is shaped and reshaped by the individuals and communities who take it up, and how playing or watching that game transforms those individuals and communities.

As an attentive spectator with a firm grip on the history of the game, he was able to bear effective witness to the outbreak of racist chanting on the Western Terrace at Headingley in 1996. The publication of his account in the *Observer* proved a powerful weapon in campaigners' efforts to chip away at the complacency of the cricket establishment. But alas, more than a decade after Chris and others began raising questions about race and racism in the game, that establishment still refuses to grapple with the issues. Casual racial and national stereotyping persists in English cricket commentary (and some coaching), as do the multiple obstacles facing grass-roots inner-city black cricketers. Yorkshire has still not promoted a locally born black or Asian cricketer to their first team. Black and working class fans in general find themselves increasingly excluded from the game's big occasions by ticket pricing and advance credit card booking.

The existence in this country of an alternative audience for international cricket - the audience about which and for which Chris has been writing - was proved by the extraordinary scenes on the final day of this year's Oval Test against the West Indies. Keen to ensure a full house for what promised to be an historic day's play, the authorities slashed ticket prices and even opened the corporate hospitality boxes to the ordinary punters. Young and old, veteran fans and first-time spectators, they poured in. For the first time all summer, black faces appeared in number. The ban on banners, flags and musical instruments was flaunted with ebullience.

It was a big day for England fans - their team's first series victory over the West Indies in 33 years. And it was a sad day for their West Indian counterparts - the definitive end of an era of inspirational cricket dominance. But all the fans were bound together in the warm tributes paid to the retiring Ambrose and Walsh. Of course, the English fans have always taken to Curtly and Courtney, unlike the English media, who until recently routinely characterised these two gentlemen as intimidating brutes. During the glory years of West Indian supremacy, Chris's was one of the very few English voices raised in celebration of that extraordinary team, that unique blend of the individual and the collective, of discipline and inspiration. In the long run, his view of this team and the forces that shaped them will win wide acceptance among students of the game, while the jaundiced whine of the contemporary English sports pages will seem an embarrassing reminder of a narrow-minded past.

Chris Searle is also one of the few cricket writers whose knowledge of the game stretches from street level to Test arena and back again. His perspective on cricket's topical controversies, as well as its deeper meanings, is informed by his experience as a teacher and active member of many communities. In the story of the Devon Malcolm Cricket Centre, Chris appears as both participant and chronicler and makes the most of the conjunction to bring out the poignancy of the tale, and its lessons for the future. If only English cricket would learn them! His enthusiasms for Viv Richards, Courtney Walsh, Wes Hall or Brian Lara are of a piece with his responses to the youngsters taking up the game in inner city Sheffield. His admirations are eclectic, unprejudiced and warm-hearted.

Chris Searle was failing the Tebbitt test with glorious aplomb long before it was even invented. These writings on cricket are but one expression of his joyous embrace of cultures of resistance, wherever they are found, and his sheer generosity of spirit.

Mike Marqusee
October 2000

# INTRODUCTION

WHY DO I GIVE SO MUCH ESTEEM to this quirky, irregular, idiomatic but profoundly beautiful game that I have known and played all my life?

It is not simply the power, idiosyncrasy and off-times grace of its choreography of white played upon green. Neither the extraordinary longevity of those who play it. I have played in or against teams who contain not only fathers and sons; but grandfathers and grandchildren too, all vitally using their bodies and brains in a complex exercise of movement and discovery. It is because cricket beyond cricket is a metaphor, a metaphysical conceit even of the processes of life. Human conflict and struggles, honour, loyalty, stamina, judgement, respect and equity are all played out on cricket pitches across the world. The play is mostly hard and unremitting, but usually generous and even comradely too: the culture of cricketers outside of the realm of money, bribe and business is frequently one that encourages the best of human skill, value and attitude.

I have been an ordinary club cricketer through most of my playing life. As a young man close to boyhood I played with my father; as a veteran now I play with my sons. The grassy, steamy Essex wickets along the London suburbs bred me as seam bowler; some basic coaching by a sometime Essex opening batsman at a rate of ten shillings a half hour at Romford indoor cricket school gave me an inveterately straight bat. The privilege of cricket: opening the bowling on a low-lying ground next to the wildflowers, reeds and mud-banks of the River Blackwater; fielding at third man alongside the crashing Caribbean surf on the village ground of Mount Pleasant, Carriacou and looking towards the scattering of the Grenadine islands; batting over an unkempt Sheffield park with a boarded-up, graffittied pavilion, or among the Derbyshire hills in Hathersage, encircled by sheep-filled meadows, oaks, a stone church and a rushing stream. This is what the game of life has offered. Or watching the glory of Viv Richards or the audacity of a Botham; the application of Laker, the rage, rhythm and sublime speed of a roused Michael Holding, Allan Donald, Waqar Younis or Wes Hall; the guile and brilliance of a Warne or Muralitharan, the all-round genius of a Sobers: that a sporting life of watching as well as playing can offer so much.

Or the metaphor turned around. The coloniser's game becoming his sporting nemesis. The cricket-playing subject becoming more than the equal, the master and destroyer too. The final blackwash. Or the revolutionary Caribbean prime minister employing the cricketing image of his people's power. 'We going to hit imperialism for six!' he declares, and then describes his nation's process of socialist emulation in the terms of a cricket match. 'That isn't cricket!' taunts the Lord's member. But it is, in a new and vibrant language, and these arrivant boys and girls in their urban Yorkshire and Lancashire streets with bat, ball and stumps painted on the Victorian brick walls which enclose their dwellings and schools, they are showing us how to play the game again.

Finally, these pages strive to release cricket from the burden of romance that has been laid across it, as a symbol of an English idyll, the enchantment of a life unshared by the millions who love and play the game. In his book *England: an elegy* published in this year of 2000, the conservative romantic, Roger Scruton, epitomised cricket in this way:

'...it displayed the reticent and understated character of the English ideal: white flannels far too clean and pure to suggest physical exertion, long moments of silence and stillness, stifled murmurs of emotion should anything out of the ordinary occur and the occasional burst of subdued applause.' (Roger Scruton, *England: an elegy*, Chatto and Windus, 2000)

It is a game that millions who play every summer weekend would not recognise. For cricket is played by real people. It is a sport of profound tensions and contradictions played by human beings wearing grubby, dirt-stained whites striped brown by dives along the boundary and in the slips and rubbed pink and bloody marks of red by the earnest shining of a leather ball. And someone launders them for the next weekend, usually a woman. It is a game steeped in conflict, aggressive speech and the ferocious shouting of appeals and commands between batsmen. Club cricketers are strongly competitive: their matches resound with 'needle' - in test matches the players 'sledge' and eyeball each other like warriors. For on the pitch of the world, we see empire, class, emerging and struggling nationhood, gender, racist contempt and racial pride playing out their antagonisms in the future of the present. I try to catch some of these moments of a sport which is still, as always, as real, unpredictable and dynamic as the loved and tended earth on which it is played.

# 1.

# RACE BEFORE WICKET
## Cricket, Empire and the White Rose
## (1990)

*'Nothing that ever came out of England has had*
*such an influence on character and nation-building*
*as this wonderful game of ours'* [1]

THUS BEGAN A VERY INFLUENTIAL BOOK on the sport of cricket, written in 1926 by M.A. Noble, a celebrated Australian cricketer who had toured England with his national team in 1899, 1902 and 1905. It was perhaps fitting that Noble should invite no less a prestigious figure than Lord Harris to contribute an introduction to his work. Harris, as well as being an ex-captain of the England cricket team, was an ex-governor of Bombay and, during his governorship (1890-95), successfully established cricket as an integral part of an imperialist culture that was designed to create a class of colonised Indians fashioned as English mimics and devotees of the Empire.

For Harris, cricket was at the centre of the imperial ideal. It represented a new way of life and set of mores which he saw as necessary to impose on the 'chaos' of India and places un-English, an approach to social organisation that combined civilised 'manliness' with teamwork and a binding respect for the hierarchy of the rule book. Cricket was an essential and symbolic part of imperial order and manners. So Harris commends Noble's book, *The Game's the Thing*, not as a sporting commentary or simply a book about cricket, but as a 'complete treatise' of 'wise advice' and

*1*

'maxims' for young people about the 'practice' of the sport and 'its etiquette, its influence and its morality'. In his own powerful way, this arch-imperialist and one man cricketing institution presaged the insight of the Trinidadian C.L.R. James some three decades hence: 'What do they know of cricket, who only cricket know?'

For cricket, being born of Empire, was also a vehicle for instituting and instilling Empire – and making clear exactly where the centre of Empire was. Even as Australia (in the absence of any black cricketing nations with national sides before the present century) became England's first and oldest 'enemy' on the cricket field,[2] cricket also reflected the imperial jingoism that infected the British people throughout the Boer wars. In 1902, the Australian cricket team touring England was the subject of this taunting little ditty in the London *Evening News*:

> *Does your circulation fail, Kangaroo?*
> *Got a frost-bite in your tail, Kangaroo?*
> *Do you find it hard to play*
> *When it's hailing half the day,*
> *And it's even cold for May, Kangaroo?*[3]

Yet for boys like myself, born into English lower middle-class households with cricketing fathers, cricket could never only be 'just a game'. It signified something overarching, religious, almost totemic, which proved you were a part of the English design. Other cultures would have ikons, crucifixes, portraits of heroes or saints affixed to their walls, An English cricketing family might have, as we did, a wooden plaque into which these words were carved:

> *And when the one great scorer comes*
> *To write against your name:*
> *He writes not that you won or lost,*
> *But how you played the game.*

That was the way it began for those within the red of the Empire: to play and love cricket wherever you lived was to believe in the spirit of England, to applaud Empire (for all cricketing countries and adversaries were Empire, whether it was Australia, New Zealand, India, South Africa, the West Indies or the newcomers of Pakistan) and to abide 'fairly' by the decisions that were dispensed by the chief umpire in the sky and mediated, of course, through Westminster.

## Imperial Illusion and Racist Reality

1989, and how has this grand imperial illusion been transformed? Fourteen English cricketers – all except one who have played for England, three of whom who have captained the national side – are, as of January, preparing to tour racist South Africa, now isolated from world representative cricket because of the campaigning energy of anti-apartheid activists and the opposition of black cricketing nations. Each player is to receive in the region of £80,000 to £100,000 for his services, with the captain, Mike Gatting, who asserts that he 'knows nothing about apartheid', reported to be receiving £200,000. As a British black player, Norman Cowans (whose county captain is Gatting himself), bowls for his county, Middlesex, against Hampshire in the semi-finals of the Nat West competition at Southampton some two weeks after the tour was announced, racist jeers of 'black bastard, black bastard' accompany his run-up. He is bowling against the South African batsman, Chris Smith. The match is being nationally broadcast live. As the abuse is transmitted across the nation and is plain to hear in living rooms from Bournemouth to Newcastle, the commentators make no comment.[4] The week before this match, Norman Cowans had bravely declared against the tour, almost a lone English professional cricketing voice: 'I think South Africa has an evil regime and I want no part of it. I would never take the South African blood money.'[5] Thus, Cowans is continuing the defiance shown by Caribbean players like Malcom Marshall and Viv Richards, who had turned down the inducements of US$1m and US$1.5m respectively, for a proposed tour of South Africa in 1984.[6]

Racism in cricket is not, of course, a new phenomenon, although insults like those hurled at Cowans have become a part of the landscape of the game only over the past decade. During the late Victorian and Edwardian eras, when the imperial torch shone at its brightest, the 'golden age' of cricket produced K.S. Ranjitsinhji and, later, his nephew, Duleepsinhji – Indian aristocrats playing for Sussex and England who, with their exotic image, had a large and popular following among British cricket lovers. One writer at the time referred to ' "the Ranji" matches, "Ranji" railway-bar sandwiches, "Ranji" bats, deckchairs, hair restorers and so forth', so great was Ranjitsinhji's fame and profile.[7] ' "Ranji" cast his magic over all his team: we saw them in the glow of his Eastern splendour.'[8] Thus wrote the most famous English cricket writer of all, Neville Cardus, in his *Autobiography*. Yet even the princely Duleepsinhji found himself barred from playing for England against South Africa in 1929 after one test match, when the South African authorities objected to his presence. As Learie Constantine, the brilliant Trinidadian cricketer of the inter-war years, later declared in his autobiography, *Cricket in the Sun*, the 'South African politicians could not face the risk of a century being scored against their team by a coloured man'.[9]

Norman Cowans, the son of Jamaican immigrants, growing up in Britain during an era of open racism – in city streets as well as government departments – also received less than 'Ranji-type' adulation at Southampton in 1989. He, too, found himself faced by something less than Lord Harris's cricketing virtues of 'etiquette' and 'morality'.

## The Caribbean game: a cricket of resistance

Cowans' principled and determined position against the degradation of his sport arises from a long struggle of Caribbean cricketers in the Caribbean itself and now in Britain.[10] It is this struggle that has been a major factor in transforming cricket from a game played and controlled by white English and colonial elites, to a sport carrying the aspirations of national independence and democratic ownership. In the Caribbean the organisation of the game mirrored the social and economic structure. From 1928, when the West Indies played their first test match against England, to 1960, when the first black captain, Frank Worrell, led the international side in Australia, white men of dubious cricketing ability had been appointed by the West Indies cricketing hierarchy as captains. This controlling coterie, composed of plantocrats, professionals and merchants, to a man white or a generous part of white, represented a class fearful of successful black endeavour. Len Hutton, the England captain of the

Caribbean tour of 1954-5, recalled how Jamaican whites drilled into the English players on the tour how important it was that they should defeat the now predominantly black West Indies side.[11] The continued supremacy of the race depended upon it. Learie Constantine had written how such attitudes and the systematic exclusion of black players with the preference for whites had 'rotted the heart out of our cricket' and hoped that 'before I die I shall see a West Indian team, chosen on its merits alone, captained by a black player, win a rubber against England'.[12]

As the black working people of the British-ruled islands of the Caribbean grew in confidence, organisation and militancy throughout the 1930s, they found their heroes and symbols on the cricket field. There was Constantine, but there was also George Headley of Jamaica, whose entry into international cricket came alongside the influence of another outstanding Jamaican, Marcus Garvey. As Michael Manley has written, Headley was 'black excellence personified in a white world and in a white sport'.[13] Headley took the black masses with him into the heart of Caribbean cricket, and the conjunction of his genius and the awakening of black resistance in Trinidad, Barbados and Jamaica in 1937-8 meant that cricket became a black man's game and the challenge was on against the white interests who controlled it. By 1950, Caribbean cricket had triumphed in the centre of Empire as the West Indies team defeated English cricket at its powerhouse, Lords. The battling trio of Everton Weekes, Frank Worrell and Clyde Walcott and 'spin twins' Sonny Ramadhin and Alf Valentine created the 'Victory Test Match' which the calypsonian Lord Beginner sang about – and which was celebrated by elated West Indians throughout the Caribbean and Britain.

> *When Washbrook's century was ended*
> *West Indies voices were blended –*
> *Hats fly in the air*
> *People shout and jump without care,*
> *Applause was the scenery,*
> *It's bound to go down in History!*

In the early 1950s, Constantine prophesied in his otherwise anecdotal book, *Cricket Crackers*, exactly how determined the Caribbean people were to become about their cricket:

> *They were still fairly patient about it but they had made up their minds*
> *that it was going to be changed even if they had to change it by strikes*
> *and other unpleasant matters…. Cricket is the most obvious and some*
> *would say glaring example of the black man being kept 'in his place', and*
> *that is the first thing that is going to be changed.*

Thus, accompanying the movements for independence in the Caribbean islands that followed during the next decade, there also came a demand for a black cricketer to lead the West Indies team. This grew to a mobilisation of press and popular support, marshalled by the Caribbean Marxist, C.L.R. James, whose *Beyond a Boundary*,[14] published in 1963, not only documented the Caribbean-wide campaign which led to the appointment of Frank Worrell as the first black captain of the regional side, but also stood as a classic statement of the link between emergent nationalism, anti-colonial struggle and sporting culture.

The popular upsurge created by these events grew stronger as the West Indies cricket team of the 1960s all but re-created the game with its phenomenal and original approach to the dynamics of the sport. Batsmen like Gary Sobers of Barbados and Rohan Kanhai of Guyana,[15] and the fast bowling Barbadian combination of Wesley Hall and Charlie Griffith – plus the off-spin of the Guyanese Lance Gibbs – established the West Indies cricket team under the captaincy of first Worrell and then Sobers as the world's strongest and most spectacular cricketing force. These were no longer the carefree 'calypso cricketers' of past caricature led by a white amateur, but a disciplined, brilliant unit led by one of their own. For what was being achieved went far beyond mere style. Here was a cricket of resistance and assertion, which mirrored an entire people coming into their own, rejecting colonial divisions imposed upon them and bringing a new confidence and will for cultural construction. Along with this capacity to improvise and forge new skills and stroke play, which characterised, for example, the batting of Kanhai, came the regional – and worldwide – creativity of the national liberation struggles, particularly those, as in Malaya, Kenya, Ghana and the Yemen, which struck out against British imperialism. In Berbice, Guyana, cricketers such as Kanhai and Basil

Butcher came out of the same mass movement (generated by Cheddi Jagan's People's Progressive Party) which also produced, for example, Martin Carter's *Poems of Resistance*. The Indo-Caribbean inventiveness of Sonny Ramadhin's left-arm spin and Samuel Selvon's nation-language novels sprang out of the same southern Trinidad. The Barbadian brilliance of Worrell, Sobers and Hall was a part of the same anti-imperialist cultural momentum that produced writers like George Lamming and Edward Brathwaite. When Charlie Griffith bowled his devastating yorkers at the English batsmen in the 1960s, they carried, too, the force of the words of Stokely Carmichael, born in Trinidad, or of Malcolm X, whose mother was a Grenadian. Lloyd and Richards were the contemporaries of Walter Rodney and Maurice Bishop; Michael Holding came from the same Jamaica as Bob Marley: their different beauties flourished during the same years.

All these associations may have been implicit, but they were expressed within the power of Caribbean cricket and its grounding principle – in Constantine's words – 'To attack is to defend.' When Gordon Greenidge, for example, set down his cultural anger, he used cricket as his form: 'I hit the ball, therefore, as a form of revenge, a personal vendetta against the ball. When I smite it into the distance I think back to all the pain I have been caused and vow to do the same to it again as soon as possible.'[16] Joel Garner, brought up by his grandmother who warned him of the class and racist forces that would be pitched against him as he grew older, saw these emerging in some of the elite administrators of the Barbadian game, and it made him determined to defeat them: 'the mysterious "they" that Gran had spoken about began to take definite shape; and although I began to grow increasingly angry at "them", I tried to break through their barriers by serious application to my game.'[17] Cricket could never be a mere pastime or weekend affectation for the black players of the Caribbean. It was a means of struggle, and achievement through it a powerful expression of Caribbean progress and nationhood.

## Blackwash

Such success made the sport even more important to the black people of the Caribbean. On Barbados beaches and street intersections, on cliffside terraces on the eastern Caribbean islands, on bush paths in Guyana – where young boys had to play straight or risk losing their ball in the thick undergrowth – cricket became even more of a regional obsession. In Petit Martinique, the second sister island of Grenada which rises from the sea rock-like and vertical, the one tiny section of flat land by the jetty and beach has been groomed into a cricket ground. The giant Barbadian fast bowler, Joel Garner, in his moving and finely written autobiography, *Big Bird Flying High,* finds that there is a little demon called 'Crickus' who lives in the heart of Caribbean life, along with the children playing with a breadfruit ball and the weekend cricketers making their pitches of dry donkey or cow manure rolled into the earth. And as Bridgette Lawrence wrote, describing the Barbadian childhood of Roland Butcher, the first black Caribbean-born cricketer to play for England, 'cricket is such a strong component of life in the West Indies that it is never far from the surface. It appears in every facet of life in the Caribbean and binds the islands together like no other force. Children are weaned on the game and it becomes imbued in the psyche.'[18]

As the West Indies consolidated their domination of world cricket in the late 1970s and 1980s, largely through the batting of Antiguan Viv Richards and Barbadian Gordon Greenidge, the skilful and unifying captaincy of Guyanese Clive Lloyd and a formidable battery of the fastest bowlers in the world – including Andy Roberts of Antigua, Jamaican Michael Holding, Guyanese Colin Croft and Barbadians Joel Garner and, later, Malcolm Marshall – they then had to face accusations that they were playing in an unfair, 'intimidatory', way. British cricket writers and administrators – in particular, after the 'blackwash'[19] victory over England in all five test matches in 1980 – began sullenly to complain that the relentless use of fast bowling by the West Indian team was against 'the spirit' of the game and was too much for an opposition to endure. They had short memories. England had won an infamous test series in Australia in 1932-3 by the 'bodyline' strategy of continuous fast bowling aimed directly at the body. The main weapon, then, was Harold Larwood, an ex-Nottinghamshire miner who was at that time the world's fastest bowler. Learie Constantine, who faced him during West Indian tours of England, wrote a rejoinder about his experiences of that era that reflected prophetically upon the fearful and sometimes racist bogus criticisms of the English critics of the West Indies speed attack that were to come in the 1980s:

*When we played Notts during that tour [1928], Larwood sent ball after ball so near our men's faces that presently some of them kept away and their wickets began to fall. We did not complain. If we could not make fours off that sort, it was our fault, not Larwood's. But we did resent the blindness of some of the critics who professed to see danger in those balls when we put them down, and none when English players bowled them.*[20]

There is no doubt that for some English and Australian cricket 'experts', sunk into the conservative traditions of the sport, the prospect of an exceptionally fast Caribbean man with a cricket ball carries the same threat as a rebellious, anti-imperial black man with a gun. They want him suppressed, disarmed – he fits nowhere into their rules and ways of the game and only challenges them. The advent of the West Indian fast bowler, from Roy Gilchrist's unfettered pace in 1957 to Malcolm Marshall's strategic, thinking deliveries in 1988, has been the most symbolically powerful image of Caribbean cricket and the triumphs of its sporting culture.

Yet there were setbacks and losses, too, within Caribbean cricket. In 1970, cricketing giant Gary Sobers, West Indies captain and the most talented all-round player the game had ever known, visited what was then Rhodesia to play in a special tournament. During his trip he met prime minister Ian Smith, at a time when Zimbabwean liberation forces were in open armed struggle against the illegal and racist regime. Sobers later claimed that he 'knew nothing of politics at the time',[21] and it took the legal skills of his own Barbadian prime minister, Errol Barrow, to try to extricate the all-rounder from international embarrassment, by writing for him a cleverly-worded letter expressing regret without apology. Then, in 1983, a group of some of the Caribbean's finest cricketers were tempted to tour South Africa, led by Lawrence Rowe, a prodigious Jamaican batsman who had scored a triple century against England. While most of the national team remained untainted, some considerable players – like Alvin Kallicharran[22] of Guyana and Collis King of Barbados – succumbed and a heavy cloud of indignation and shame fell over the region's cricket: South Africa's destabilisation of black people crossed the Atlantic and infected the Caribbean.

The most positive response came from Grenada's revolutionary government during its last year of life, which, while 'condemning this treacherous sell-out to the oppressors of our brothers', recommended that all Caribbean governments, as well as cancelling immediately the passports of the mercenary cricketers, should 'confiscate on their return the earnings from the South African venture and turn this over to the African National Congress (ANC) and the South West African People's Organisation (SWAPO) to help finance the anti-apartheid and national liberation struggle in Southern Africa'.[23] Such exemplary measures were not taken, despite the regional sense of disgust and betrayal, but future attempts at recruitment of some of the most talented Caribbean cricketers were roundly rejected. It is to the eternal credit of players like Joel Garner and Malcolm Marshall – both of whom had known very little money in their families and who had spent their youth, as Marshall put it, 'unemployed with no realistic chance of getting work'[24] – that they rejected such corrupting propositions as those made to them by officials of the white South African Cricket Union.

## The bite of Apartheid

If the South African overtures created confusion and some betrayal within the structures of Caribbean cricket, the few black British cricketers playing in the English county championship were even more isolated and vulnerable. Surrounded by white team-mates, many of whom coached and played regularly in South Africa during the winter months with the full encouragement of their own Cricketers' Association,[25] and subject to the racist taunting of crowds in places like Leeds, Northampton and Southampton, they lacked the racial and cultural solidarity of their Caribbean counterparts. The humbug 'morality' preached by Lord Harris was nowhere to be seen. In 1981 Geoff Boycott, the Yorkshire batsman who scored more runs in test cricket than any other Englishman, publicly promised Indian Prime Minister Indira Gandhi during the English tour of India in 1981 that he would never play in South Africa again. Even while he was actually making this promise, Graham Gooch writes in his book, *Out of the Wilderness*,[26] Boycott was arranging recruitment, with clumsy subterfuge, for the subsequent 'rebel' tour of South Africa (which included Gooch himself, as captain) a few months later.

The organisation of the tour, financed by the Holiday Inn hotel multinational (which also has powerful interests in the Caribbean), reads like the plot of a spy novel, with the top English cricketers all being clandestinely approached, and (according to Gooch) only David Gower and Ian Botham turning down the offer because of principled positions against apartheid. Feted, wined and dined in 'five-star comfort' by the white racist elite of South Africa's cricketing establishment and paid £45,000 each for their 'work', this was what Gooch called the 'big, brave concept' of breaking through the cultural and sporting boycott of South Africa. Gooch sought to vindicate himself by declaring that he was simply a cricketer pursuing his trade, that there was generally strong support in England for him (illustrated by right-wing parliamentarians like Lord Chalfont, the South African government's most prominent House of Commons lobbyist, John Carlisle MP, and the 'Freedom in Sport' organisation). He also claimed that he was snubbed by the 'coloured' cricketers represented by the South African Cricket Board – an affront he described as a 'reversal of apartheid' – and, anyway, why give more than a thought to the black population, for to 'suddenly hand over control to the blacks could create a situation of pure farce'.

It is not just that black cricketers have to play alongside and against men with such views, but that the English cricket authorities appoint them as captains of their national team – as Gooch was appointed in 1988. John Emburey, also a profiteer of tours to South Africa and an active campaigner for Margaret Thatcher's Conservative government, was appointed during the same season.[27] Under such pressure, two black British cricketers, Roland Butcher (who plays in the same county team, Middlesex, as Gatting and Emburey) and Philip de Freitas, were tempted to join Gatting's party to South Africa in 1989. But, responding to the counter-pressure of indignation across British black communities (with Cowans playing an important persuasive role in the case of Butcher, his Middlesex team-mate), the two players withdrew just over a week after the touring party was announced. The incident demonstrated, however, the influences that surround black players in the English county game.

While these events were happening, a delegation from South Africa's Mass Democratic Movement (including Krish Mackerdhuj, president of the South African Cricket Board) arrived in England to attempt to persuade Gatting and his party to pull out of the tour. 'Our message is simple', they said. 'These tours will set back our efforts to develop non-racial sports. They will give comfort to the apartheid regime and its supporters. They will undermine our struggle to create a non-racial and democratic South Africa.'[28] Bill Morris, the black deputy general-secretary of the British Transport and General Workers' Union, wrote an open letter to Gatting. It declared: 'If you decide to go to South Africa, the hurt that will cause to the opponents of apartheid and the damage it will do to the prospects of other sportsmen will never be forgiven or forgotten. It will permanently overshadow your success on the cricket-field. Is that how you would really wish to be remembered?'[29]

Meanwhile, anti-apartheid activists picketed cricket grounds at Sheffield, Cheltenham, Derby, Southampton, Lords itself and other venues where the cricketers from the touring party were playing, and the people of South Africa, through their own Congress of South African Trade Unions (COSATU), continued with their campaign of defiance of apartheid's racist laws. As South African police arrested 113 women hospital orderlies during a Cape Town protest on 22 August and tear-gassed a peaceful demonstration of black children, a union spokeswoman – being dragged away to detention – spoke out: 'We are protesting against our pay, against the way they treat us like dogs and against the government's plans to make worse laws against the Trade Unions.'[30] On the same day, the tour organisers secured another recruit, Greg Thomas, the Northants fast bowler. 'It will be a big disappointment not to be able to play for England,' he was quoted as saying – referring to the ban against representing England for five years imposed against the tourists by British cricket authorities – 'but financially there was no question what to do'.[31] It was an echo of the contention of Yorkshire fast bowler Paul Jarvis: that he had to go on the tour, because he needed the money to pay off the mortgage on his new house. That was the present condition of Lord Harris' vision of the 'etiquette, influence and morality' of the imperial game.

## Black newcomers

With the exception of the Caribbean islands and the *maidans* of Indian cities like Bombay, there is probably no place in the world where cricket is played with so much fervour as in the counties of Lancashire and Yorkshire, in the north of England. Lancashire, in particular, has attracted a large number of black players who have been employed as professionals for the league clubs. From Learie Constantine employed at Nelson in 1929 to Viv Richards at Rishton in 1987, the Lancashire leagues have been ambivalent hosts to black players. Constantine played when it was a rarity to find black cricketers, indeed black people, in the cotton towns of Lancashire. Although he encountered 'colour bars' in hotels and racist petulance among cricket administrators, he found the people warm and hospitable and, when he decided to leave, 'could not walk half a mile in the streets without being stopped literally hundreds of times by all sorts of people I didn't know from Adam: men, women and even youngsters begging me to stay'.[32] The Nelson Old Prize Brass Band rendered 'Abide with Me' for Constantine in the interval of Nelson's first match after his decision to leave the club was announced. But that was the era when a black cricketer was an exotic, unthreatening figure. By the 1960s, when immigration acts, emergent fascist groups and Enoch Powell were beginning to make life harder for the larger numbers of black people in the north of England, conditions were somewhat different.

In 1960, Basil D'Oliveira, a cricketer from Cape Town who was classified by the apartheid apparatus as 'coloured' and who had achieved brilliance while playing on the rough matting pitches of the 'coloured' League of West Province, arrived in England. After the intervention of cricket commentator John Arlott, amongst others, he had been offered a contract playing as a professional for Middleton, in the Lancashire League – which was worth £450 for the entire season. When it was discovered that he still had to find £200 for his passage, his fellow cricketers in Cape Town banded together to collect enough money to make it possible for him to reach England and start a professional career. This was to take him eventually to county and international level (as a player for England, of course, not South Africa) and he became the reluctant catalyst for South Africa's eventual isolation from world competitive cricket when its government refused to accept his inclusion in the English touring side of 1968. In his autobiography, D'Oliveira explicitly denied he was writing a 'political' book – as Arlott wrote in the introduction, 'any time since 1960 a single word from him on apartheid would have been dynamite'.[33] But his book tells of the 'unrelieved depression' of trying, as a black stranger to England and English cricket, to cope with his new conditions in the northern industrial town that was his new home. 'I could think of nothing else except hide', he wrote. And later, when his wife arrived to join him and they would go to the cinema, he was always conscious of hostility from the people around him: 'We always thought they were staring at us and muttering to each other: "What are those people doing here?" Often my right arm would have bruises the following morning where my wife gripped me so hard.'

## Keeping the White Rose white[34]

Yorkshire has proved to be an even more unwelcoming territory for black cricketers. For, unlike Lancashire, whose county side has frequently included black players like Patrick Patterson from Jamaica and Wasim Akram of Pakistan and whose captain for a number of years was Clive Lloyd, Yorkshire County Cricket Club retains a birth qualification which has helped to exclude black players from selection for the 126 years of its history. As Neville Cardus (a Lancastrian) once wrote: 'The joke about Yorkshire cricket is that for Yorkshiremen it is no laughing matter. It is the possession of the clan and must on no account be put down, or interfered with by anybody not born in the county.'[35] In a post-imperial era, where much of the chauvinism of Empire and nation has been transferred to a regional or city jingoism – which itself has been fanned through the parochial fervour of football team worship – the notion of Yorkshire 'birthright', far from withering away, has grown stronger. In 1987, the rumour that the Yorkshire club was considering 'signing' West Indian captain Viv Richards to play for the county side was greeted by aghast ex-Yorkshire cricketers like Fred Trueman as a crime. Trueman later threatened to tear up his membership card of the county club if an 'overseas' cricketer ever played for Yorkshire.

In his history of Yorkshire cricket, *We Don't Play it for Fun*,[36] author and cricket commentator Don Mosey reveals the archaic yet still current bigotry that lies behind this notion of the 'clan'. Speaking as a Yorkshireman, Mosey muses: 'If lesser mortals, unfortunate enough to be born on less hallowed ground, do not really understand this point of view, then that's their problem.' Calling Yorkshire players 'the chosen people of cricket.....the pleasure has come from being the best', Mosey's rhetorical humour is at least half-serious, and illustrates the restrictionism and narrowness of mind that is fertile soil for racism. This became clear in the particularly crude terms of Yorkshire MP John Townend in August 1989, as the fascists of the British National Party were planning their anti-Muslim march through Bradford. Speaking of the British Muslims who had protested against the publication of Salman Rushdie's *The Satanic Verses*, Townend declared: 'They should be told they have the answer in their own hand – go back from whence you came.' He continued, 'Have we been so debilitated that the English have lost their voices and no longer think of themselves as the sole possessors of England?'[37]

On the day the 1989 tour of South Africa was announced, Ray Illingworth, ex-Yorkshire and England captain, revealed another ugly aspect of this institutionalised prejudice: 'We've been dictated to by these countries overseas for too long. I don't blame these players, they have to look after their families and their own future.'[38] The same week, a group of Yorkshire football supporters, wearing the colours of Leeds United, were seen fleeing from the scene of a murder of a young Spanish waiter, Jesus Moreno, in San Antonio, Ibiza, a favoured haunt for drink-crazy young 'Brits' who proudly wear T-shirts with such legends as 'You Hate Us, and We Don't Care' and whose holiday pleasure consists of fomenting drunken brawls, vandalising streets and restaurants and insulting local people.[39] This brutality of thought has also found its way on to the Leeds cricket terraces at the county ground of Headingley. Viv Richards was almost brought to resist physically the racist insults hurled at him there when playing for Somerset against Yorkshire in 1986, and in the previous season, black Gloucestershire and England fast bowler David Lawrence described the hostility he met there from the local Yorkshire crowd:

> It makes me sick when I hear Yorkshire committee men saying they have the best, most loyal supporters in the world; that there weren't any racist fans in the crowds. It's absolute rubbish. I was standing on the boundary line and there was a whole section calling me all the names under the sun. They called me nigger, black bastard, sambo, monkey, gorilla, they threw bananas and I had take these insults.

While playing against the Australians at Bristol during the same summer, he received a letter with a Yorkshire postmark which declared: 'Don't shout yer mouth off nigger, you won't be welcome next time, Nig Nig.'[40]

Such sentiments, of course, are not restricted to Yorkshire cricket supporters. In Bradford, a city close to Leeds, Asian young people have been brought to using cricket bats as a means of self-defence against groups of marauding white youths who have threatened their neighbourhoods and screamed abuse at their community.[41] The point is that the institutionalised Yorkshire chauvinism, such as that proclaimed through the 'birthright' policy of Yorkshire cricket, buttresses the root causes of such violence and racism. There has never been a black person who has played for Yorkshire. You need to have been born in the county. Thus, the thousands of young black people who have come to live within its boundaries, having been brought there as children by their immigrant parents to live in places like Leeds, Sheffield, Bradford, Huddersfield, Dewsbury and Halifax – even if they had arrived in these cities as babes in arms – are barred from playing cricket for Yorkshire. Even though exceptions have been made for aristocrats who captained the county side like Lord Hawke (born in Lincolnshire) and a number of other players, there is no room for black Yorkshire residents born outside Yorkshire. Devon Malcolm, who came to live with his family in Sheffield from Jamaica when he was 16, and who went to a local college and played cricket for a local club, had to 'cross over' the county boundary to play county cricket as a fast bowler for Derbyshire, from where he gained international recognition for England in August 1989.

Such a situation is absurd and tragic, not only for black young people within the county growing up as Yorkshirewomen and Yorkshiremen, but for Yorkshire Cricket itself. For its players in the past were instrumental in transforming the game from the property of the southern aristocrats and middle classes into a sport with a genuine working-class orientation. Whereas in southern England, cricket is still mainly the preserve of suburbanites and men in white collars in Yorkshire it is a game loved and played predominantly by working people, organised through leagues and village and works sides. Players of extraordinary and original ability like George Hirst and Wilfred Rhodes – both from the village of Kirkheaton near Huddersfield, the first who worked as a wirer for a hand-loom weaver and then in the dye-works, the second as a railwayman before turning professional – contributed to changing the entire character and constituency of cricket in the early part of the twentieth century.[42] Unfortunately, they, and hundreds of other players like them, including Sutcliffe, Leyland, Hutton and Fred Trueman from the mining village of Maltby in South Yorkshire, never challenged the Yorkshire chauvinism so embedded in its county cricket.

## A part of the struggle

The first black cricket players that caused interest in Yorkshire were the members of the Australian Aboriginal side who toured England in 1868. When they arrived to play a match at York, they were excluded from the luncheon tent on the grounds of race. A contemporary balladeer turned this event into verse:

> *Now Gents should be Gents and not snobs,*
> *But I am sorry to say,*
> *The Yorkists refused the blacks to lunch*
> *Until they done that day...*[43]

Although 'this untoward event was the cause of much criticism and many comments', as a Yorkshire contemporary wrote, it set the direction for the relationship between Yorkshire County Cricket Club and black cricketers which in some basic ways has not changed since.

In August 1989, David Sheppard, the Anglican Bishop of Liverpool who played cricket for England during the 1950s, wrote the following about South Africa in *The Cricketer*:

*Any substantial numbers of boys cannot have facilities because the Group Areas Act confines black people, coloured people and Asian people to inadequate land. Providing good cricketers needs an unbroken chain – boys' cricket, village and park cricket, good club cricket, first class cricket. Those of us who have lived and worked in the inner cities in England know how difficult it is to give opportunities to boys in areas where good club cricket is only to be found at a distance in another kind of suburb.*

*17*

Sheppard is correct to liken the situation in South Africa to Britain in this regard. In the inner-city areas of England, where black young people are most numerous and their appetite for cricket is at its strongest, resources for the sport are at their most pathetic. Only one in twenty schools in inner London, for example, plays regular inter-school cricket fixtures and there are few innovative attempts by local councils to remedy this. A notable exception is the Haringey Cricket College, which has developed a number of talented young black cricketers of both sexes.[44] Recently, I played a match in a neighbourhood park in Sheffield where the majority of residents are of Pakistani descent. Of the twenty-two players and two umpires, all were white, while the vast majority watching were black young people. The Yorkshire club's claim is that such people have 'a certain insularity'[45] that stops their involvement in the leagues. Brian Close, one of its most famous committee members and another ex-county and England captain, tells black cricketers that they 'must integrate into the top leagues'.[46] Yet, when the Yorkshire County Cricket Club opens an 'Academy of Cricket' in Bradford, despite the thousands of black Yorkshire youngsters, many of them with a deep attachment to the game - particularly those from the Indian, Pakistani and Caribbean communities – no black prospect could find a place amongst the eleven apprentices initially taken on at the 'Academy'. And this, even though clubs like Hanging Heaton have produced very talented black players, through the coaching of professionals like prominent international stars Abdul Qadir and Dilip Vengsarkar.[47] Thus, when journals like the *Sheffield Weekly Gazette* blandly declare that 'There are no charges of racism to answer. Rather, there is some dismay at Headingley that no coloured player has yet proved good enough to graduate to county level',[48] they receive a cynical response by black cricketers, as do the promises of 'ethnic days' for talent-spotting, to be organised by the Yorkshire county club.

The 'integration' arguments have proved very unconvincing. In its efforts to join the South Riding League, Sheffield's Caribbean Cricket Club has been turned down *twice*. First, it was told that its pitch was not up to the standards of the league. Then the league, satisfied with the pitch at last, decided that the *team* itself was below standard, even though, in its second letter of application, the club secretary maintained that in recent years at least six of the club's players had been transferred to clubs playing in division one of the league, and two others had moved straight into the stronger Yorkshire league, with one of these going straight on to play for Derbyshire in the county championship. Neville Roe, a white businessman who has supported and sponsored the Caribbean CC, is very critical of the way in which the league and its white clubs treat black players: 'They will accept a couple of blacks in the team – like a quick bowler or a fast-scoring batsman – but it seems to me that there is prejudice against a whole team of blacks playing and socialising in their own way.'[49] When Paul Miller, a Caribbean CC player, joined the prestigious Sheffield United Club and became its sole black player, he felt estranged and neglected – as he had when he was the only black member of the Yorkshire Colts side: 'I was just there to make up the numbers. I never got any encouragement or coaching. I was never welcome.'[50]

With this pressure, it is not surprising that talented black players living in Leeds, who play for regular league sides on Saturdays, prefer to play in their own league – the Quaid-e-Azam League – on their Sundays. Likewise, Owen Gittens of the Caribbean CC asserts that 'Sport is a very important way in which we can improve the lot of our own people',[51] and the club has become the fastest-growing sports club in Sheffield.

The daunting obstructions faced by black sporting organisations like the Caribbean CC are not restricted to bureaucratic obstacles, lack of interest, discouragement and non-recognition of their players' talents. In 1987, a series of attacks on their newly-established ground in Ecclesfield near Sheffield began. First, the new clubhouse windows were smashed, then broken glass was scattered over the pitch. In 1987, an arson attack caused £8,000 worth of damage to the roof and the club tractor was destroyed. Then, in 1988, the club scorebox was also burned to the ground. The groundsman, who has worked at the ground for thirty years, had never before encountered trouble of this kind.[52] Although the South Yorkshire police dismissed these attacks as 'petty vandalism', Caribbean CC member and local council race equality officer Mike Atkins concluded that they were further evidence of the 'endemic racism' in Yorkshire and its cricket. This attitude continues within the ruling circles at the county club level. The *Yorkshire Post* reported on the club's October 1989 general committee meeting in the following way: 'In the "out tray" went Captain Phil Carrick's proposal to strengthen the team by signing players from outside the county boundaries. There was no support at all for an overseas import, and there were only three representatives in favour of signing "foreigners" born in England.'[53]

Yet, despite – and because of – the history of this most contradictory and ambivalent of games, black cricketers all over the world play on, at the most basic but most essential level of their clubs and leagues, sparking an essential part of their national culture – whether in Karachi, Barbados, Soweto, Sydney or Yorkshire. For those communities in struggle, cricket – the imperial game – is transformed and becomes part of the struggle.

**REFERENCES**

[1] M.A. Noble, *The Game's The Thing* (London, 1926)

[2] Despite the white-managed tour of black Australian cricketers to England in 1868, Australian cricket teams were composed of cricketers from white-settler backgrounds.

[3] Percy Cross Standing, *Anglo-Australian Cricket 1862-1926* (London, 1926)

[4] Almost all the English radio and television cricket commentators have cordial links with South Africa and its white cricket authorities. Jack Bannister managed the first unofficial tour of white cricketers after South Africa was banned from the international arena in 1968; Trevor Bailey and Fred Trueman have featured on promotional videos for the white South African Cricket Union and Christopher Martin-Jenkins was Master of Ceremonies at one of their banquets; Tony Lewis has broadcast for the South African Broadcasting Corporation. Brian Johnston, the veteran radio commentator, announced Gatting's tour on the 'Test Match Special' (1 August 1989) by declaring: 'They are merely following their profession' (see John Booth, 'The Voice for South Africa', *Cricket LIfe Interantional* (October 1989))

[5] *Daily Express* (10 August 1989)

[6] Malcolm Marshall, *Marshall Arts* (London, 1987)

[7] Percy Cross Standing, op.cit.

[8] Neville Cardus, *Autobiography* (London, 1947) (

[9] Learie Constantine, *Cricket in the Sun* (London, 1947)

[10] Another voice of protest has been that of Gladstone Small, the black Warwickshire and England fast bowler, who criticised other cricketers who 'don't really consider the wider issue of oppression' in South Africa (*Cricket Life International* (October 1989))

[11] Len Hutton, *50 Years in Cricket* (London, 1984)

[12] Constantine, op.cit.

[13] Michael Manley, *A History of West Indies Cricket* (London, 1988)

[14] C.L.R. James, *Beyond a Boundary* (London, 1963)

[15] For an instructive description of Kanhai's cricketing genius, see Birbalsingh and Schiwcharan, *Indo-West Indian Cricket* (London, 1988)

[16] Gordon Greenidge, *The Man in the Middle* (London, 1980)

[17] Joel Garner, *Big Bird Flying High* (London, 1988)

[18] B. Lawrence and R. Butcher, *Rising to the Challenge* (London, 1989)

[19] During the last test match of the 1980 series at the Oval Cricket Ground in London, Caribbean supporters produced a large banner ironically proclaiming BLACKWASH across it. In cricket parlance, 'whitewash' is when a team suffers a loss in every match of a test series.

[20] Constantine, op.cit.

[21] Garfield Sobers, *20 Years at the Top* (London, 1988)

[22] In August 1989, Kallicharran himself became the target of racial abuse from sections of the crowd whilst playing for Warwickshire at Northampton (see *Daily Mail* (4 August 1989))

[23] Quoted in Chris Searle's *Grenada Morning* (London, 1989)

[24] See Marshall, op.cit. and Joel Garner, op.cit.

[25] The Cricketers' Assciation - the 'trade union' of English cricketers - was put on a firm financial footing after receiving cash from the Transvaal Cricket Union in 1973. Over 100 current members have passed their winters and supplemented their incomes, either playing or coaching in South Africa. Neal Radford of Worcestershire and England, for example, has played for both Transvaal and the South African Army (see *Cricket Life International* (October 1989))

[26] Graham Gooch, *Out of the Wilderness* (London, 1985)

[27] Gooch was re-appointed, this time to lead the English tour of the Caribbean during the winter of 1989. On the day of his appointment (8 September 1989) twenty-five black South Africans were killed in Cape Town as they protested against the 'whites only' national elections.

[28] *Morning Star* (19 August 1989)

[29] Ibid.

[30] *Morning Star* (23 August 1989)

[31] *Guardian* (23 August 1989)

[32] Constantine, op.cit.

[33] Basil D'Oliveira, *An Autobiography* (London, 1968)

[34] The White Rose is the traditional emblem of Yorkshire and Yorkshire County Cricket Club.

[35] Cardus, op.cit.

[36] Don Mosey, *We Don't Play it For Fun* (London, 1988)

[37] *Guardian* (29 August 1989)

[38] Spoken on Test Match commentary, BBC Television ( 1August 1989)

[39] *Daily Telegraph* (7 August 1989)

[40] *Daily Mail* (12 August 1989)

[41] *Guardian* (11 Jul;y 1989)

[42] See A.A. Thomson, *Hirst and Rhodes* (London, 1959)

[43] John Mulvaney and Rex Harcourt, *Cricket Walkabout* (London, 1988)

[44] See articles by B. Lawrence in *Cricket Life International* (September 1989)

[45] *Independent* (3 June 1989)

[46] Spoken on 'Sportsnight', BBC Television (8 June 1989)

[47] *Independent* (3 June 1989)

[48] *Sheffield Weekly Gazette* (20 July 1989)

[49] *Independent* (6 February 1989)

[50] *Mail on Sunday* (30 April 1989)

[51] *Independent* (6 February 1989)

[52] *Sheffield Star* (19 May 1987)

[53] *Yorkshire Post* (12 October 1989)

# 2.

# CRICKET AND THE
# MIRROR OF RACISM
## (1993)

IF POPULAR SPORT CAN BECOME THE MIRROR of the attitudes within a society, the reporting of it in a press which itself poses and parades as 'popular' can make that reflection even more lucid.

This was illustrated with powerful truth during the English summer of 1992, by the way in which the British press reported the cricket test match series between England and Pakistan. Coverage of this major sporting event grew to a frenzy during the last days of August. As Mike Selvey, the cricket correspondent of the *Guardian*, put it, it was 'the biggest witch hunt in the game' for thirty years.[1] So much so, that in parks and on cricket fields all over Britain, Pakistani cricketers – boys and men – became the targets of crass sniggers and insinuations about being 'cheats' and 'ball doctors' as they went about playing and trying to enjoy their national game, or simply picked up a ball in order to bowl.

All through the summer, Pakistan's brilliantly effective pair of fast bowlers, Wasim Akram and Waqar Younis, accounted time after time for the English batsmen with bowling of exceptional skill and outstanding late swing.[2] The response from a battery of British sports journalists was an attempt to undermine their achievement by labelling them as cheats and covert rule-breakers. This journalistic campaign came to a climax on 26 August, when English cricketer Allan Lamb – who had been born and bred in apartheid South Africa but who had qualified to play for England from 1982 onwards and had played seventy-nine times during the following decade – launched an attack on Wasim and Waqar in the mass circulation *Daily Mirror*. He accused them of cheating and of transgressing Law 42.5 of the Laws of Cricket by 'doctoring' the ball by scuffing it up one side, so as to increase its capacity for late and prodigious swing in the air in unexpected directions. Under a banner headline proclaiming them the 'cheats of Pakistan', Lamb's article claimed that Wasim and Waqar 'gouge the damaged ball with their nails, then smear the surface to fool the umpire',[3] cosmetically covering up the cracks and tears they have made in the leather by smoothing them down with their sweat.

With the *Mirror* cricket correspondent Colin Price writing that 'Pakistan's cheating cricketers fly out of England today – as free as birds',[4] implying that they had done something that warranted their being detained, and a *Mirror* editorial writer declaring that there should be some sort of deportation order issued against them – 'The Pakistan team should be drummed out of England in disgrace'[5] – a storm of hostility broke across the British tabloid press. The *Mirror* led the attack, proclaiming Lamb a hero and insulting the two Pakistani bowlers in particular, dressing them down as scoundrels and cheats who will be remembered 'by many for their tricks and tantrums'.[6] On it continued, day after day, in words and pictures. 'It's just not cricket!' exclaimed the caption on a Griffin cartoon in the *Mirror* of 27 August, portraying Waqar, with pliers and screwdriver stuck inside his belt, bowling a gouged-up ball to an English batsman, which swings in all directions and ends up chasing two terrified pigeons.

## From the *Sun* to the *Mirror*

This was not the first time that the British tabloid press had mounted a campaign of hostility against Pakistani cricketers and cricket officials. In December 1987, after an angry on-field conflict had developed between Mike Gatting, the English captain (who was to lead a 'rebel' tour of South Africa during the winter of 1989-90, reportedly earned £200,000 for his work and finally got a five-year ban from test cricket as his reward), and Pakistani umpire Shakoor Rana (called by the *Sun* 'the crackpot of Karachi') during the Second Test Match at Faisalabad, *Sun* journalists had pitched in, leading a tirade of abuse and invective, labelling the umpire as a cheat. This chorus had continued for several days, with a *Sun* editorial complaining that 'our boys out there are being cheated left, right and centre by the Pakistanis'. A banner headline screamed 'Pak yer bags!' and, after the tour was completed, the leader writer commented: 'Thank God the tour of Pakistan is over at last. If our cricketers never want to see the bloody place again, who can blame them?'[7]

The *Sun* had exercised a malevolent leadership over the story, building in and extracting as much racist content from it as it could, and inflaming anti-Pakistani feeling among white readers in Britain with relish. Now, in August 1992, it seemed that the tawdry mantle had been passed to the *Mirror*, which had learned from its rival's methods during the course of the circulation war being waged between the two dailies. Certainly, in the space that it devoted to the 'doctoring of the ball' story and the way it set out purposefully to pillory Wasim and Waqar and lionise the eager Lamb, the *Mirror* was doing much more than merely emulating its gutter-mate.

The *Mirror* had already foreshadowed its methods in the treatment it gave to the 1991 West Indies cricket tour to England. At the tour's outset, Colin Price had written a back-page headline story claiming to be 'a damning verdict on the West Indies'. The huge letters proclaimed 'Accused', with, under portraits of the Caribbean cricketers, the words: 'They are the most unpopular team in the world. Their game is built upon vengeance, violence and arrogance.'[8]

These words had been taken from an article in *Wisden Cricket Monthly* (which claims to be, as a part of the legendary 'Wisden' tradition, a revered source of authority to cricket-lovers) by its Australian editor, David Frith. The *Mirror* reprinted almost all of Frith's caustic article, which was a follow-up to the hostile and vituperative campaigns waged by the British sporting press against West Indies touring sides of previous years, when their own phenomenally fast and skilful bowlers, like Malcolm Marshall, Curtley Ambrose, Michael Holding and Joel Garner, had consistently devastated brittle English batting (as Wasim and Waqar were to do in 1992). In 1987, on the West Indies' previous tour, the *Sun* in an editorial had told the Caribbean cricketers to 'Stay away. Permanently.' It had attacked them for supporting an international ban on cricketers who had boosted the apartheid system by playing in South Africa.[9]

The *Mirror's* 1991 attack on the Caribbean players centred upon their captain, Viv Richards, who was accused of gamesmanship, intimidation and being 'at the very centre of the war-dances'. The 'serious' papers, too, had their daggers out, with the *Guardian*'s Matthew Engel attacking the Antiguan for his 'assertions that Caribbean cricket represents black aspirations', which, Engel claimed, had 'caused great offence' to Caribbean people of Indian descent in Trinidad and Guyana. Biting deeper, Engel went on to condemn Richards for his consciousness of history, complaining to a predominantly white readership that Richards

> *seems to be carrying the whole burden of history on his shoulders. You might think he blames every white man he sees for the deforestation of Antigua for sugar cane (which makes it horribly drought-prone) and what Sir Christopher Codrington, the chief local slave-owner, might have done to his great-great-great-great-great-grandfather.*[10]

What is noteworthy, in retrospect, about the 1991 reporting is the way it is echoed in the 1992 columns, with the *Mirror*'s vanguardism in the attacks on the Pakistanis being reinforced by the 'heavies'- including those newspapers like the *Guardian* with reputations for liberalism and 'fair play'. The *Mirror*, unlike the *Sun* (which is an avowedly Tory newspaper, bringing the Conservative racist message unambiguously to British working people), proclaims itself a 'Labour' newspaper. And yet, as this latest attack on Pakistani sporting success and achievement shows, its treatment of such issues reflects a similar jingoism to that of the *Sun*.

## 'National character' and British press racism

For those who regularly read the sporting press in Britain, particularly the *Mirror*, the declining days of the 1992 cricket season were redolent with the portrayal, in banner headlines, of 'the guts of Allan Lamb', plus other stories continually reiterating the 'guilty-by-cheating' accusations against Wasim and Waqar. In a speech bubble superimposed over a full-page colour photograph of both Pakistanis in the *Mirror* of 31 August, they are shown exclaiming: 'It wasn't me – it WASIM!' The story was dubbed by Colin Price as 'the great Pakistan ball-doctoring scandal', even though no evidence beyond Lamb's accusations was ever brought forward as proof. Despite the *Sun*'s hostility towards its arch-rival, the *Mirror*, it, too, was not slow to make a hero and a martyr out of Lamb. 'Good on yer Lamby!' it announced in its 'Sunsport' issue editorial of 27 August, adding weight to Lamb's claim by its own characteristic abuse of Pakistan as 'a bunch of ball-gouging cheats'. The previous day's edition had included an interview on the controversy with Bob Wills, another ex-captain of England, who seemed to reach his own ugly conclusions, not only about Pakistani cricket, but about the Pakistani national 'character' too:

> *It's just the way the Pakistanis are brought up to play their cricket. It's the nature of the beast. Everything is confrontational. They don't say sorry willingly and don't often accept they are in the wrong....it's not part of their character.*[11]

These judgments, leading from comments on cricket to declarations about the 'national character' of Pakistan, were not limited to the tabloid press. The *Guardian's* Michael Henderson, in his column of 10 August, took the words of the internationally respected cricket commentator, John Arlott, that 'cricket reflects the personality and spirit of those who play it, and by extension, illuminates the national character', and twisted them to his own ends by adding that 'all summer long the Pakistanis have been wilful, capricious and hot-headed'.[12]

The conception of cricket as a form of culture which expressed a people's uniqueness and strength of creative development was, of course, one entertained by great cricket writers like Neville Cardus and C.L.R James. In *Beyond a Boundary*,[13] James luminously showed how Caribbean cultural and political resistance, the consolidation of regional unity and confidence, and the determined opposition to racism had been fused around cricket in the campaign for, and final selection of, Frank Worrell as the first black captain of the West Indies cricket team in the late 1950s, but what was being expressed about the Pakistanis in these peevish judgments by English ex-cricketers and journalists in the British press was a national caricature, not national character. They were seen to be condemning not only Wasim and Waqar, but the entire Pakistani people – including the large, English-based community which was on the receiving end of increased racist violence in the streets and estates of Britain's inner cities. For, as Ian Wooldridge – typifying the press response and writing in the *Daily Mail* –

declared, the 'volatile' Pakistani cricketers had provoked an affair which 'hangs like an ugly thundercloud over a team, a *nation* and a game of presumed integrity (my emphasis)'.[14] It was unlikely that such a press was going to condemn its own provocateurism and baiting of the Pakistani team and its so-called 'national character'. One writer took this to an extraordinary socio-biological level by moving from national character to national perspiration – concluding that what made the crucial difference with Pakistanis were 'the certain properties in their sweat which achieve a superior polish' when the bowlers shine up the ball on their cricket whites to gain extra swing.[15]

## Fighting back, and other voices

The Pakistanis were not slow to defend themselves against the British press's own 'presumed integrity', and answered the vituperation with a combination of rectitude, pride and disappointment. Wasim and Waqar were clearly saddened that out of their own English team-mates – with whom they had played on a day-in, day-out basis during previous seasons in Lancashire and Surrey, respectively, and with whom they had achieved notable success in the English County Championship and one-day competitions – none came forward to defend them or said anything to dispel the ugly accusations. 'Both Waqar and I have played a lot of county cricket and nothing has been said about our bowling until this summer. Why is that?' asked Wasim,[16] who continued by saying that he believed the accusations were motivated by racism and colonial rivalry. 'They taught us cricket', he added, 'but now that we are winning, England are bad losers.'[17] Intikhab Alam, ex-captain of Pakistan and now manager of the international side, asserted: 'Our achievements this summer have not been tainted by these allegations. We have far better bowlers, everyone accepts that. These stories are all rubbish.'[18] Of Lamb's accusations, he continued: 'I think this is a very cowardly attack', and, suggesting a build-up of racism behind the South African's actions, added, 'There is something behind this, I don't have to spell it out – it's very obvious.'[19] Yet the mere accusations seemed enough to goad Lieutenant-Colonel John Stephenson, secretary of the International Cricket Council, the controlling body of the game, to declare, blimpishly,: 'We are determined to stamp out this sort of thing!'[20]

In the wake of the chorus of bitterness against Pakistan's cricket, however, new evidence began to emerge and new voices to make themselves heard across the cricket establishment. The Australian ex-test match batsman, Bob Cowper, who had been match referee for the first two test matches of the summer between England and Pakistan, was tracked down holidaying on the French Alps. When asked for his opinion on the controversy, he gave it unambiguously: 'During those games I personally examined the balls after each session of play. None had been tampererd with. I have no explanation as to why Pakistan's fast bowlers can consistently get an old ball to swing so much. They just do. Maybe,' he added with a smile, 'it's because they're very good bowlers indeed.'[21] Simon Hughes, a county cricket circuit veteran now playing for Durham, came clean when he wrote that 'the reverse swing phenomenon is not a new discovery', adding that it had been used regularly by the great Pakistani fast bowler, Imran Khan, all through the 1980s. 'He used various fingertip skills,' wrote Hughes in the *Independent on Sunday*, 'some of which he demonstrated, others he guarded. One of these seemed to be to manoeuvre the quarter seam so it acted like a rudder, pulling the ball in the different direction it was intended.' Almost from nowhere, the creative genius of Pakistani cricket and its ability to improvise new skills for new conditions was being acknowledged and 'discovered'. Hughes went on to say that one of the blue-eyed young men of English cricket, Angus Fraser, regularly scuffed up the ball while bowling, and that 'the secret of this whole issue is to avoid discovery. At all levels of English cricket, slip fielders have lifted the seam, so much so that at times you might cut your fingers on it. There are several first-class players who have imparted oily substances from their clothes onto the ball, and one team used non-scented talcum powder.'[22] The hypocrisy behind English cricket and its press guardians came teeming out.

Imran himself came forward in the *Daily Telegraph* to describe, quite concretely and without defensiveness, the reverse swing technique – explaining it as a response to the specific conditions of pitches in Pakistan. 'We in Pakistan have been practising it for years', he declared:

*Our grounds are hard and our wickets bare. Consequently the ball gets scuffed up within a few overs. There is no great secret to it. Once the ball*

> *is rough and one side is dampened and polished, then the ball will swing*
> *towards the polished side, as opposed to the conventional way in England*
> *where it swings opposite to the polished side.*[23]

Such techniques of dampening the ball with natural sweat and polishing it
to create a shine on one side were, of course, entirely within the rules of the
game and used by weekend, school and club cricketers the length and
breadth of England (and regularly by the present writer too!) As *Guardian*
writer Mike Selvey had already written in his report of the Fourth Test
Match on 10 August:

> *There is nothing sinister in all this. If fast bowlers are to be a force in*
> *Pakistan, where the conditions reduce the new ball to the texture of a*
> *pair of Hush Puppies in the space of a dozen overs, they need something*
> *more than seam or Cherry Blossom shine that English greenery and*
> *fertilised outfields maintain here. So, necessity being the mother of*
> *invention, Sarfraz Nawaz in the seventies devised a method of lending*
> *bias to the ball – in the manner of a bowling wood – by using sweat and*
> *spittle to soak one side. The process was refined by Imran Khan and now*
> *has been perfected by Wasim and Waqar.*[24]

What also began to emerge – beyond a gathering understanding of the
Pakistani's abilities to confront and overcome cricketing problems within
their own environment – were plain facts that showed that other
international sides were themselves tampering with and damaging the ball
to help their bowlers, long before the victorious Pakistani team was reviled
by the British press in the summer of 1992. In 1990, for example, New
Zealand medium-pace bowler Chris Pringle bowled out Pakistan in a test
match and had admitted to shredding the leather cover of the ball with a
bottle top that he had secreted in the pocket of his cricket trousers.

## The truth emerges

Finally, even the *Mirror* and Colin Price – the main protagonists of the
controversy- had to admit, in the paper's banner headline of 1 September
that 'They're all at it!', quoting the words of Sir Colin Cowdrey, chairman

of the International Cricket Council, with stories of the England team itself being reported to test match umpire John Holder in 1991, for scuffing up a ball during the previous summer's final test against the West Indies. The English test batsman David Gower revealed in his autobiography[25] (which was hurried into publication during the week following the outbreak of the controversy) that he had complained about the Indian bowlers 'scuffing up' the ball during the Oval Test of 1990, when he had scored an unbeaten century. Now, even the motives of Allan Lamb, who, as Mike Selvey had written, had enthusiastically taken on 'the mantle of the protector of cricketing morals', were at last put to question, with Scyld Berry of the *Independent on Sunday* suggesting that the South African's eye was 'on the main chance', and that although he might appear to be martyring his own cricket career, his ambitions was, in fact, to represent his country of birth, now being allowed back into the international cricket arena.[26]

Throughout this affair, Mike Selvey of the *Guardian*, writing with the breadth of understanding of his great predecessor, Neville Cardus, was the one British cricket journalist who appeared to appreciate that cricket, like any other popular cultural activity, is dynamic; that it changes according to conditions and the ways in which the most talented and creative players can respond to those conditions. English players had learned to lift the seam of the ball to cause it to deviate sharply off grassy wickets; the technique learned and adopted by the Pakistanis was much more applicable to hard, virtually ungrassed surfaces. Now the latter technique had been successfully applied to English conditions by Wasim and Waqar. The additional factors included their sheer pace, with the ball coming towards the batsman at the speed of 90 miles per hour, their devastating use of the 'yorker' which came swinging in, bouncing towards the batsman's toes, the clever variability of the pace of their bowling and their outstanding accuracy. All this made their fast bowling the most accomplished in the world. They were simply the best.

It took some honest letters-to-the-editor, published right across the political spectrum of the British press, to put the truth of the matter most cogently. Writing to the *Daily Telegraph*,[27] R.E. Hargreaves of Cumbria exposed the hypocrisy of the English county game by showing how nobody from Surrey or Lancashire (the English county sides that Waqar and Wasim play regularly for) had complained of their techniques when both bowlers had achieved outstanding results for them during previous seasons. He also quoted from the cricketing 'Bible', *Wisden*, whose 1992 year book had included a statement from the Surrey county coach, Geoff Arnold, attributing Waqar's success to his skill in using the shiny-rough contrast of the older ball and to a 'greater ability to swing the ball late and at a faster pace – not to mention landing it in the block-hole – more than anyone I have seen'. Keith Flett, an irrepressible letter-writer who writes at least a letter a day to British newspapers, wrote to the *Morning Star*: 'England cannot stand being beaten by a former colony and when they are, accusations of cheating begin to abound.'[28] And Tawhid and Nahid Ahmed, writing to the weekend edition of the *Daily Jang*, the high-circulation Urdu daily read widely by the Pakistani community in Britain, reinforced this argument: 'They could not face it that a country which is very much hated by the English, actually beat them at their own game.'[29] But then, as a CARF correspondent pointed out, England had 'learnt on the playing fields of Eton' how to 'keep on changing the rules so that you keep on winning'.[30]

But, by the time such reflections were being published and the truth behind the controversy was being revealed, forcing its way through the prejudices of the tabloid journalists, the damage to Pakistanis living in their homeland, and living in a new homeland in England, had already been done. A British mass circulation newspaper (and this time a self-proclaimed 'Labour' one), for the second time in five years, had led a scurrilous, vicious and subliminally racist campaign against the Pakistani people, choosing that people's national success in sport against their old colonising power as its vehicle. And, during that same summer, within six weeks of one another, three Asian men had been murdered, the victims of racist violence in Britain – Ruhallah Aramesh in Thornton Heath, Ashiq Hussain in Birmingham and Rohit Duggal in Greenwich. At the very same time that the 'ball tampering' controversy was being stoked up in the *Daily Mirror*, with its millions of white readers, another Asian youth was shot at point-blank range and blinded in one eye by a racist gang in Harrow, north London, and a mosque, a Sikh temple and a Hindu gurdwara were fire-bombed and attacked in south London.[31]

The specific relationship between such ugly and murderous racist behaviour and its encouragement through distortion, invective and racist targeting in the populist sports journalism of the national tabloids may be impossible to determine accurately. But that it lends its weight to further acts of violence and malice by those goaded by twisted headlines and simplistic jingoism is as evident as it is pernicious. For such journalism is a mirror of daggers.

**REFERENCES**

1 *Guardian* (27 August 1992)

2 For an informative account of the careers of Wasim Akram and Waqar Younis up to 1992, see John Crace, *Wasim and Waqar: Imran's Inheritors*

3 *Daily Mirror* (26 August 1992)

4 *Daily Mirror* (29 August 1992)

5 *Daily Mirror* (26 August 1992)

6 *Daily Mirror* (25 August 1992)

7 The *Sun's* coverage of this incident and its aftermath are documented in Chris Searle, *Your Daily Dose: racism and the Sun* (London, 1989)

8 *Daily Mirror* (23 May 1991)

9 *Sun* (15 June 1987)

10 *Guardian* (1 May 1991)

11 *Sun* (26 August 1991)

12 *Guardian* (10 August 1991)

13 C.L.R. James, *Beyond a Boundary* (London, 1963)

14 *Daily Mail* (26 August 1992)

15 *Independent on Sunday* (30 August 1992)

16 *Star*, Sheffield (19 August 1992)

17 *Star*, Sheffield (27 August 1992)

18 *Yorkshire Post* (25 August 1992)

19 *Star*, Sheffield (26 August 1992)

20 *The Times* (26 August 1992)

21 *Daily Mail* (26 August 1992)

22 *Independent on Sunday* (30 August 1992)

23 *Daily Telegraph* (31 August 1992)

24 *Guardian* (10 August 1991)

25 David Gower, *The Autobiography* (London, 1992)

26 *Independent on Sunday* (30 August 1992)

27 *Daily Telegraph* (31 August 1992)

28 *Morning Star* (28 August 1992)

29 *Daily Jang* (2 October 1992)

30 'Is it cricket?'. *CARF* (No. 10, September-October 1992)

31 See *Anti-Racist Alliance Bulletin* (October 1992)

# 3.

# LARA'S INNINGS
## A Caribbean Moment
## (1995)

*I tole him over an' over*
*agen: watch de ball, man, watch*
*de ball like it hook to you eye*

*when you first goes in an' you doan know de pitch.*
*Uh doan mean to poke*
*but you jes got to watch what you doin;*

*this isn't no time for playin'*
*the fool nor makin' no sport; this is cricket!*

Edward Brathwaite: *Islands* [1]

ON 18 APRIL 1994 AT ST JOHN'S, ANTIGUA, Brian Lara, a young Trinidadian cricketer, knelt and kissed its Caribbean earth, and his people rejoiced.

He had gone beyond the furthest boundary, scoring 375, more runs in a single innings of an international match than any previous player, with a powerful one-footed pull that crashed the ball against the legside boundary fence. The man whose score he had surpassed, the Barbadian Gary Sobers, walked out to the centre of the ground and embraced him. Antiguans and other Caribbean people watching the drama engulfed and feted him and his young Indo-Guyanese batting partner, Shivnarine Chanderpaul. The Antiguan police, called out to control them, guarded Lara like a 'national treasure',[2] while joining in the celebrations of a scattered nation finding its centre. For this nation, Lara's kneeling to the earth was more than an act of patriotism: it was a sacred moment. The team of the old colonial power, defeated by Lara's strength, creativity and epic concentration, stood around the Antiguan field and beheld.

The team of the Caribbean, watching from their pavilion, marvelled and celebrated: from Jamaica and Guyana, from Barbados, Antigua and Trinidad. Also, there was wicket-keeper Junior Murray, the first Grenadian to be part of a West Indies test side. In the midst of this joy, the words of Lara's late countryman, C.L.R. James, from *Beyond a Boundary* blew in the sea breezes across the Antigua Recreation Ground: 'What do they know of cricket who only cricket know? West Indians crowding to tests bring with them the whole past history and future hopes of the islands.'[3] For Brian Lara had done more than all the imperial ritual re-enactments of Columbus's 1492 landfall upon the Americas, staged across the region two years before, could ever accomplish. He had touched the collective Caribbean brain and heart of a dispersed people and fuelled their unity and hope. As the Barbadian Brathwaite had written over two decades before, the spectacle of cricket had provoked a sudden new regional pride and confidence – as it had done at Lord's in 1950 or after the 'Blackwash' of England in 1980:

*All over do groun' fellers shakin' hands wid each other*
*as if was <u>they</u> wheelin' de willow*
*as if was <u>them</u> had the power.*[4]

## The context

More needs to be said about the particular context of this moment in the Caribbean. The young black Englishman, Chris Lewis, who had bowled the ball to which Lara had swivelled and then pulled decisively to the legside boundary for his record score, was himself from an Afro-Guyanese familyy of the diaspora. One of Lewis's team-mates, Mark Ramprakash, was a

Londoner whose father is Indo-Guyanese. Watching from the English dressing-room, and foolishly omitted from the team by the English selectors, was a man born in Jamaica whose family emigrated to Sheffield in Yorkshire – Devon Malcolm. According to the great Jamaican fast bowler, Michael Holding (now retired and writing in the regional cricket journal), Malcolm was the one English bowler who had threatened Lara's ascendancy in a previous test match encounter, exposing a 'delectable flaw' in Lara's failure to deal with the sheer pace and 'line of attack' of rising balls coming in towards his body.[5] Thus, the Caribbean was unequivocally a part of English cricket, too. Like the English health and transport systems, it could not function effectively without the essential Caribbean contribution. Lara's achievement had also been integrally linked to the diaspora: it was something much more than a routine meeting of two sporting nations; it transcended a historically-charged confrontation between the ex-colonisers and the decolonised. Now the Caribbean was on both sides.

This truth was exemplified most forcibly during England's final test match against South Africa (now readmitted into international cricket after the end of formal apartheid) in August 1994. Along with Devon Malcolm's match-winning bowling of nine wickets for fifty-seven runs in the second innings, which, in Malcolm's own words, 'made history', of the still all-white South African team, nineteen of the twenty South African wickets fell to bowlers of Caribbean origin. In the October 1994 issue of *Wisden's Cricket Monthly*, normally a staunchly establishment journal, a poem called 'Irresistible', written by one Paul Weston, was published. Referring to the 'whipped-up cream of Devon', the poet ingeniously contrived the following verse:

> *For every Bok who took a lick*
> *Was rendered copiously sick,*
> *Their faces whiter than their shirts*
> *Struck down by Malcolm's just desserts.*

Such admiration from the white sports media was unusual for a black cricketer who, as Stephen Brenkly of the *Independent on Sunday* had put it, 'had been written off more times than he had been written up' and who, at a function at Buckingham Palace in 1991 when both the West Indian and

England teams had been invited, had been asked by the Duke of Edinburgh himself, 'Why are you wearing an England blazer?'

In *Beyond a Boundary*, James had written of the pioneer English cricketer, W.G. Grace, that he 'was strong with the strength of men who are filling a social need.' If only the old agitator could have seen Lara's innings and experienced its impact within Trinidad and across the Caribbean! As Lara returned to Piarco airport in his home island on the night after the test match ended, a huge crowd awaited him. Prime Minister Patrick Manning called it a 'redletter night' and the next day was designated 'National Achievement Day', with all schools having a holiday and Lara traversing the two-island state in a motorcade. President of Trinidad and Tobago Noor Hassanali presented him with the Trinity Cross, the highest national honour. An elated prime minister also announced that he could have a house of his choice, and a street in Independence Square, Port of Spain, was renamed 'Brian Lara Boulevard'. Lara, like James a boy from a small settlement in the hinterland, was presented with the keys to the city by the mayor of Port of Spain. And all this in a country that has often been slow to give public recognition to its own great national figures, such as its writers James and Selvon. In these scenes of festivity, Lara travelled side by side with his team-mate, Chanderpaul, making a tableau of Afro-Caribbean and Indo-Caribbean unity against the communalism that has often plagued political progress in Trinidad and Guyana. It was a felicitous public expression of James' assertion in *Beyond a Boundary*: 'The cricketer needs to be returned to the community.'

And this community was a regional and international one wherein the shout of Maurice Bishop could be heard: 'One Caribbean!' The Barbadian daily paper *Nation* printed on its front page a photograph of Sobers with an affectionate arm around Lara's shoulders, and wrote in its editorial: 'In years to come, Caribbean people of this period will refer to the events of yesterday at the Antigua Recreation Ground with great relish and pride. The distinction of being the scorer of the highest individual number of runs in a test match was transferred from the shoulders of our own Sir Garfield Sobers and now rests on the shoulders of our own Brian Lara.'[6] In Jamaica, Tony Becca, cricket correspondent of the *Gleaner*, wrote: 'When, years from now, the fans talk about the highest individual innings of all time... they will remember the strokes that glittered in the Antiguan sunshine. What will keep flashing in the mind's eye forever were the drives and cuts, the hooks and pulls of Lara, strokes which sparkled like diamonds and which will also last forever.'[7] The Antiguan socialist and cricket enthusiast, Tim Hector, wrote in the *Outlet*:

> *What an event Lara's innings was – the acuity of mind, the athleticism, the economy of movement and motion, using the bat for his brushwork, a bat commonly used by boy and girl. Boy and girl in the Caribbean, and maybe well beyond, will be lifted to new heights, for Lara is the beginning of something new.[8]*

Island and race, nationality and gender suddenly fused in these words of a Caribbean morning, and cricket was their spur. And the words followed the diaspora. The most commonly published photograph of the Antiguan events across the world where cricket is played was of Lara kissing the pitch. 'Sealed with a kiss' headlined the London *Daily Mail*, and Australia's Adelaide *Advertiser* declared, 'Lara's greatness sealed with a kiss'. In Canada, the Toronto *Star* highlighted the innings, and even across the USA, where cricket is a relative rarity, Caribbean migrants and exiles could read about Lara in *Newsweek* or *Sports Illustrated* and watch the news of his achievement on the CNN cable network. In England, even that habitual peddler of sporting racism, the *Sun*, suddenly and uncharacteristically changed from vulgarity to a more sophisticated, even poetic, mode:

> *...he shattered one of the oldest and most majestic records in sport, he made the world stand still. He temporarily cleared troubled minds of war and want, of conflict and poverty, prejudice and greed. He deals in numbers beyond the imagination, the comprehension and reach of almost every batsman who has lived... Go and see him, watch a genius at work.[9]*

It was as if Lara's batting had also transfixed what Bishop used to call the 'saltfish' establishment press of the Caribbean, as well as strangely affecting the tabloid mammoths of the old seat of empire.

Other more authentic voices across the Caribbean and through its diaspora communities were raised in praise of Lara. Writing to the

*Caribbean Cricket Quarterly* and island newspapers were cricket-loving letter-writers from across the region, from Dominica to Montego Bay, from New Amsterdam in Guyana to Belize. Many of these correspondents praised Lara as an example to Caribbean youth, as a role model in a region sinking deeper into US cultural influences and a drugs ethos. From Edwin Scott in Penal, Trinidad, came typical sentiments:

> *What impressed me most about Brian Lara's great innings in Antigua was not his strokes or his concentration. What I found very revealing was the tributes he paid to those who helped him in his career and how he made special mention of his parents and his family.*
>
> *A lot of young sportsmen tend to get very swell-headed and self-centred when they achieve not a quarter of what Lara has. He is an example to all our youth, not only in the way he bats but the way he conducts himself.*[10]

## Filling the need

Yet in more than a cricketing sense, Lara's innings – all 768 minutes of it – had come with a deep breath of relief across the Caribbean. Starting to bat from what Barbadian cricket writer Tony Cozier called a 'base of potential crisis',[11] he had rescued the West Indies' first innings in Antigua after the loss of two early wickets – while facing the aftermath of the previous test match which had been lost in Barbados. This was but the microcosm on the cricket field of a more general social crisis, for there were wider and deeper sloughs that the Caribbean people and their progressive spirit had been mired in over the previous decade. The revolutionary defeats and setbacks suffered in Grenada and Nicaragua, the tightening squeeze of the US upon Cuba, the collapse of the Left in Jamaica and its weakening in Trinidad were all lodged within the consciousness of the region. And, in Lara's homeland, the violent and futile lunge at power in 1990 by the Jamaat-al-Muslimeen sect had followed months of humiliating exposures of rampant corruption at the government level, in the shape of the Tesoro scandals.[12] The Trinidadian soca artiste, David Rudder, had satirised such sordid depths in his 'Panama', singing of those who made their dishonest thousands and then moved elsewhere to spend and benefit from them:

> *Dem rich Trinidadians show me*
> *Dis whole El Dorado ting*
> *Dey say dey living here like lords*
> *But den dey gone to live there like kings*
> *As dey get a little money in dey pocket...*[13]

It had been ten years of US domination, through IMF and World Bank structural adjustment packages and attacks on local dependent economies, as well as cultural offensives through religious evangelism, tourism, food, music and information. And there was also what Tim Hector called 'the increasing influence of Americanised sport in the region'.[14]

Rudder had seen this loss of strength directly manifested in cricket. In his calypso, 'Rally round the West Indies', he had related it to externally organised attempts to confuse and divide Caribbean people by insularity, 'conflict and confusion' – as well as the making of new 'restrictions and laws' to undermine directly the West Indies' cricketing strengths, particularly the efficacy and power of its squad of fast bowlers. Yet, even in 1988, he could point forward to a cultural breakthrough through cricket, remembering James:

> *in the end we shall prevail*
> *this is not just cricket...*
> *This thing goes*
> *Beyond the boundaries*

and could even anticipate the new era of Lara and the devastating Antiguan fast bowler, Curtly Ambrose, another destroyer of English cricket hopes in the Caribbean in 1994:

> *Pretty soon runs will flow again like water*
> *Bringing so much joy*
> *To each and every son and daughter*
> *So we going to rise again like a raging fire*
> *As the sun shines*
> *You know we got to take it higher!*

When James wrote that 'if and when society regenerates itself, cricket will do the same', he gave an implicit message to the Caribbean people: watch your cricket, study it too, for it will tell you where you are and where you could go. This is not a fiction – so integral is cricket to the national spirit of the English-speaking Caribbean. It gives the one enduring image of unity and aspiration, as well as inter-island cooperation. It is also an emblem, almost an icon, across Caribbean life that has been rendered even more powerful by the spectacular contribution of Lara. When the Barbadian government came to present an official gift to the first legitimate president of South Africa, Nelson Mandela, upon his inauguration in May 1994, it was an oil-painting depicting Sobers driving a cricket ball. Even the baseball-loving Fidel Castro became involved in the cricket life of Cuba's sister islands in April 1994, during a visit to Barbados for a UN conference on sustainable development for small island states. *Caribbean Cricket Quarterly* described this bizarre yet unifying event in its region's cultural history:

> *As his entourage drove past a ground in the Holder's Hill district on his way to the Sandy Lane Hotel where he was staying, Castro ordered his car's driver to stop. He got out, an aide went onto the field to speak to the umpires and it was agreed that the famous and unexpected guest could have the chance of playing the game for himself. Play in the Barbados Cricket League match between St John the Baptist and Police was temporarily halted. Castro, in military uniform, faced and missed three balls from a Police bowler and bowled a couple of deliveries before thanking his hosts and taking his leave.[15]*

## Inventiveness and concentration

If there were two particular qualities that marked Lara's innings in Antigua directing the Trinidadian's speed of wrist and hand, they were confidence and concentration.[16] During the 1993 tour of Australia, Lara had scored 277 at Sydney and caused Sobers to change his mind about whether his record score could ever be passed. There were few batsmen playing, he had declared, 'with the necessary depth of concentration to stay at the crease for ten hours or more and aim for a score of 300 plus'.[17] After watching Lara bat at Sydney, he thought again. For Lara, and particularly for his mother, confidence was not a problem. Pearl Lara saw her son's innings as ordained, as a gift of God, and remained utterly unsurprised by his achievement, declaring that she knew it would happen from when he was a boy. Lara himself had remained composed all through his time at the wicket, building his score consciously, fifty by fifty, his confidence being expressed in the way that he described his reaction to the ball that gave him his record-breaking boundary. Recalling Lewis's bowling approach to him, he said: 'The minute I saw him running in to bowl that ball, the energy I saw him putting in – I kind of predicted it was going to be short. I latched on to it pretty early and got it away.'[18] As for concentration, Michael Holding compared Lara with the great Caribbean batsman of the previous decade, Viv Richards of Antigua. Whereas 'Lara still manages to keep his concentration no matter what his score, and never seems to become distracted', Holding sees Richards' genius as more adventurous and less disciplined: 'After he had been out in the middle for a few hours doing as he pleased, he would start looking to do something different and lose his wicket through carelessness.'[19]

These two, often counterbalancing, approaches to Caribbean cricket have also formed a dialectic for decades. They fascinated James, who knew that studying the way a people played their cricket meant that 'much, much more than cricket is at stake'. His friend, collaborator and great Trinidadian all-rounder, Learie Constantine, personified the creative genius of the Caribbean and its cricket in the years between the two world wars. Utterly inventive in his approach to batting, he made brilliant strokes with 'no premeditated idea' of making them, and thus continued a tradition in Trinidad begun by Wilton St Hill who, to the cricket-loving people of his island, was 'our boy' in the way that Lara is today. According to James, St Hill would 'invent' a stroke on the spot – like Rohan Kanhai and his falling-down pull of the 1960s – and Constantine added that this 'slender boy flashed his wrists and the ball flew to the boundary faster than sound'.[20] Yet in international cricket, St Hill failed sadly and Constantine, despite his snatches of brilliance, never scored a century in a test match and could not sustain his domination over the bowling for long periods. James knew that with such erratic cricketing talent the Caribbean was 'still in the flower garden of the gay, spontaneous, tropical West Indians'. And, he added wryly, 'we need some astringent spray'. That came initially with the concentrated and disciplined batting of the Jamaican George Headley during the 1930s, and was followed by the 'Three Ws' – Weekes, Worrell and Walcott – in the 1950s, by Sobers and Kanhai in the 1960s, and Greenidge, Lloyd, Richards and Haynes in the '70s and '80s. But the apotheosis of Caribbean batting stamina, as well as creative confidence in the fierce pulling, hooking, powerful cuts and drives, has come with the 375 runs in Antigua of Brian Lara. His innings provides an image of relentless application and will, of concentration and colossal physical and mental effort. 'I believe every great batsman is a special organism,' pronounced James, and Lara has become a living symbol of dedicated striving, fused with a virtually peerless technique, that will serve towards countering the self-critical fear in the Caribbean – made, for example, by the Barbadian cricket spectator in Brathwaite's 'Rites'. This is the fear that continued in the wake of the murder of Walter Rodney, the self-devouring collapse of the Grenada Revolution after so much promise and achievement, and the violent fiasco in Port of Spain's Red House in July 1990 when the Muslimeen attempted their futile coup:

> *when things goin' good, you cahn touch*
> *we, but leh murder start*
> *an' ol man, you cahn fine a man to hole up de side...*[21]

## Lara and Caribbean hope

Writing in the *Outlet*, Tim Hector invested Lara's innings with the heraldry of a profound hope and optimism. He recalled the all-round brilliance of Sobers and his 365 against Pakistan in Jamaica in 1958 as a product of the Caribbean federal and liberating impulse of the time – which gave birth to the short-lived West Indian Federation, the Cuban Revolution of 1959 and the cultural flowering of Naipaul, Wilson, Harris and Lamming in literature and the Mighty Sparrow in calypso. And he pointed towards a new era signalled by Lara's achievement:

> *I would want to think that Lara's innings put behind us the conditionalities of the IMF with its structural adjustment that has structured Caribbean people out of their own economy and history. They*

*will return centre stage after Lara because Caribbean history can be divided into BL (Before Lara) and AL (After Lara).*

*After Lara, there will come in this part of the world a new creative impulse, rejecting the Ramboisation of life and living which now plagues our cracking or crumbling economies.*[22]

Optimism indeed, but not groundless optimism, for these are the thoughts of a tireless Caribbean activist, a veteran doer who knows well his people and his culture. Those who do not know cricket and its beckonings and symbols may well say to themselves or each other, 'What is all this?' But, as James wrote and Hector knows, others, like Frank Worrell, the first regular black captain of the West Indies, have 'cleared the way with bat and ball' for the struggling people of the Caribbean, and new cricketing generations will do likewise in completely new contexts. The key to Hector's hope lies in James's assertion that 'the cricketer needs to be returned to the community' – for there are many alternative forces waiting to comsume such talent as that of Lara and the temptations of big money are enormous and potentially corrupting, as Caribbean cricket already knows well. They destroyed the previous West Indies triple centurion, the Jamaican Lawrence Rowe, who became a Caribbean hero after his innings of 302 against England in Barbados in 1974. Rowe took the repugnant step of leading a cricket tour to South Africa and promoting apartheid by breaching the sporting boycott of the racist regime. Now Brian Lara is the hottest potential acquisition in world cricket, and companies across the Caribbean and beyond are thrusting to sponsor him and milk his achievement. His prodigious batting exploits while playing English county cricket for Warwickshire during the summer of 1994, including the highest ever individual first-class cricket score (501 made against Durham at Edgbaston in June 1994), have made him even more of a prize for multinational corporations. Early contracts promoting Coca-Cola and '501' jeans presage one potentially dangerous direction – the ordinary people of the Caribbean and its diaspora, their hopes and aspirations, stand on another road and they have claimed Lara as their own. He is 'their boy' and his bat strikes for their future.

But the temptations towards a multi-faceted exploitation of Lara's achievement, in a US-dominated carnival of profit and graft, are only too real and enticing for those in the *comprador* economies of the Caribbean. It is a true test match for cricket, as well as for Lara. For if sport, particularly a sport so integral to the regional psyche as cricket is to the Caribbean, is to remain, as James saw it, both a spur and reflector, and not a deflector, of political and social reality, it must stay close to the people, to the community of those who love it and play it on recreation grounds and pitches improvised from pastures in villages all through the English-speaking Caribbean, to those who have transformed it from the imperial game and made it their own. If not, it becomes for that same community what Learie Constantine once wrote it could be, 'a hasheesh… a drug in their poverty-stricken and toiling lives'[23] – not the mirror which James saw into, but a clouded glass that reveals only cultural theft and the oppression of the new imperialism of the north.

## A place in the world

As Lara played his innings in Antigua, another pathmaking Trinidadian died on their island. This was Sam Selvon, novelist, playwright and short story writer, of whom James said, 'He has an ear for the West Indian language, the West Indian speech that is finer than anything that I have ever heard.'[24] In the 1950s, Selvon's writing, in particular his re-creation of the ordinary speech of Trinidadians at home and as arrivants in London, had broken through the imposed, 'correct' and often lifeless version of English spoken and vindicated by the coloniser and his education system. The real world of Trinidad's people and their creole tongue – its images, its wit and tenderness, its beauty, energy and irrepressible national spirit – burst through in the narrative of Selvon's works: *A Brighter Sun* (1952), *The Lonely Londoners* (1956) and *Ways of Sunlight* (1957). Like Lara's cricket, his writing was made in the bloodstream of the Caribbean, in the villages 'behin' God back' like Cantaro, near Santa Cruz, Trinidad, Lara's own birthplace. As one of Selvon's characters expounds in his play *Highway in the Sun*:

> *Whatever it is, what do you expect to happen in this half-dead village? One day just like another. Is only in England and America big things does happen.*[25]

But every village has its cricket pitch, has its young people that can be other Brian Laras. That is what Selvon teaches us, and James too – the boy who formed his politics watching village cricketers like Matthew Bondman and Arthur Jones through his parents' bedroom window, cutting and driving on the recreation ground outside – that everywhere there is excellence and power in the ordinary, in the community of humans, in the languages that they speak and in their bodies which they move for work, pleasure and achievement. It had been the working-class Australians of town and outback who had adopted Donald Bradman as 'their boy' and their living anti-colonial symbol after his record-breaking scores of the early 1930s. Like the cricket lovers of Antigua who ran onto the pitch in a passionate embrace as Lara kissed the ground in April 1994, sealing what T.S. Elliott once described as 'the intersection of a timeless moment',[26] so thousands of working people in London, like my father, also fled from work and risked a sacking to see Len Hutton, a shy 21-year-old batsman from a Yorkshire village, score the final runs to overcome Bradman's record score at the Oval in the summer of 1938, on the threshold of war against Hitler, and then to see Bradman, with the same 'grace and consideration'[27] as Gary Sobers, shake Hutton's hand in the middle of the pitch.

But back to Selvon, for his death upon one Caribbean island coincided with a massive blast of life upon another. The Trinidadian novelist, Earl Lovelace, another beautiful user of his people's language as expressed in *The Dragon Can't Dance* or *The Wine of Astonishment*, who helped to clear the trail blazed by Selvon, takes up the narrative:

> *Sam had talked almost in a voice of bewildered hurt of what he was seeing in Trinidad. Something had gone dreadfully wrong. And that is why I believe it must have given him great pleasure and renewed hope that at his passing the young batsman Lara was playing his historic innings in Antigua. I don't think it's out of place to claim that as a stone in the monument for a man whose work was one of the earliest expressions of the West Indian's unconditional self-confidence and demands for a place in the world.*[28]

For that is what Brian Lara's success truly signified, like Selvon's liberation of language, Bishop's and Rodney's struggles or James's lifetime of luminous insights, an 'unconditional self-confidence and demand for a place in the world'. And those who will follow and emulate Lara's innings must strive to transform his moment into their era.

## REFERENCES

[1] Edward Brathwaite, 'Rites' from *The Arrivants: a New World Trilogy* (London, 1973)

[2] Ian McDonald, writing in *Caribbean Cricket Quarterly* (Barbados, July 1994)

[3] This and other quotations from C.L.R. James come from *Beyond a Boundary*, republished in 1994 by Serpent's Tail, London.

[4] Brathwaite, op.cit.

[5] See *Caribbean Cricket Quarterly* op.cit.

[6] *Nation*, Barbados(19 April 1994)

[7] *Daily Gleaner*, Jamaica (19 April 1994)

[8] See article by Tim Hector in *Lara: 375* (Barbados, 1994)

[9] *Sun* (19 April 1994)

[10] *Caribbean Cricket Quarterly* op.cit.

[11] Ibid.

[12] See Chris Searle, 'The Muslimeen insurrection in Trinidad' in *Race amd Class* (Vol. 33, no. 2, 1991)

[13] See booklet with David Rudder's lyrics with compact disc, *Haiti* (London, 1988)

[14] *Caribbean Cricket Quarterly*, op.cit.

[15] Ibid.

[16] Qualities that the Hampshire captain, Mark Nicholas, had seen as an expression of Lara's 'outstanding cricketing brain'.

[17] *Lara: 375*, op.cit.

[18] See Reds Perreira's interview with Brian Lara in ibid.

[19] *Caribbean Cricket Quarterly* op.cit.

[20] Quoted in C.L.R. James, op.cit.

[21] Brathwaite, op.cit.

[22] Tim Hector in *Lara: 375* op.cit.

[23] Learie Constantine, *Cricket Crackers* (London, undated)

[24] C.L.R. James in an unpublished interview with Chris Searle (London, 1983)

[25] Sam Selvon, *Highway in the Sun* (Leeds, 1991)

[26] T.S. Eliot, 'Little Gidding' from *Four Quartets* (London, 1959)

[27] Ian McDonald, op.cit.

[28]From an article by Jeremy Taylor, 'Ply it again, Sam'. *BWee Caribbean Beat* (Trinidad, 1994)

# 4.

# TOWARDS A CRICKET
# OF THE FUTURE
# (1996)

FOR THE THIRD CRICKET TEST MATCH against the West Indies, played at Edgbaston, Birmingham, in July 1995, England fielded an all-white side for the first time for several seasons. This exclusion of black players ended a period when their contribution to the national team had become routine, as well as entirely justified. At the final test match against the residually white South Africa in August 1994, nineteen of the twenty wickets to fall were taken by bowlers of Caribbean origin, including Devon Malcolm's match-winning 9-57 in the second innings (the fourth best-ever bowling performance by an English player in all international cricket), and Joey Benjamin's four wickets in South Africa's first innings, which gave a strong foundation for the England victory. Now suddenly there was no Malcolm, no De Freitas or Lewis, Small, Ramprakash or Nasser Hussain. Other black players who had become what the cricketing press called 'one-test wonders', dropped after single appearances and creditable performances and never to be recalled – such as Neil Williams or the recently very effective Benjamin – were also absent from the line-up.

This new lilywhite team was selected at a particular conjunction of events and issues in British political and sporting life which conferred a certain significance upon it. The first signal came through an article by Robert Henderson in the prestigious establishment cricket journal, *Wisden Cricket Monthly*.[1] Claiming to deal with the issue of cricket and national identity, this theme soon reveals itself to be but a fig-leaf for a series of racist assumptions and myths. Declaring that non-English born players are likely to fail Norman Tebbit's infamous 'cricket test' (you are only truly English if you support England at cricket when they are playing against the national team of your country of origin, be it Pakistan, Sri Lanka, India or the West Indies), Henderson comments: 'It is difficult to believe that a foreign-born has any sense of wanting to play above himself simply because he is playing for England.' He also asserts that the oppression and exploitation of Empire and colonialism are 'post-imperial myths' purveyed by 'Negroes' and 'Asians' and, within cricket circles, by liberals and 'coloured England-qualified players'. The essay provoked widescale news and television coverage, particularly when Malcolm and Phillip de Freitas, cricketers playing for Derbyshire, launched a legal case against it, with the full support of their county cricket club and the Professional Cricketers' Association.

The provocative and rhetorical title of Henderson's article, 'Is it in the blood?', his preoccupation with the idea of the 'unequivocal Englishman' and his final summing up – 'All the England players whom I would describe as foreigners may well be trying at a conscious level, but is that desire to succeed *instinctive*, a matter of Biology? [author's emphasis] There lies the heart of the matter' – stretch his fancifulness into the area of racist genetics. The pseudo-scientific question, 'Is it in the blood?', brings back strong memories of a book I read as a boy, the autobiography of the one-time captain of the South African test team, Dudley Nourse. *Cricket in the Blood* it was called.[2] From start to finish, in this book, written by a man who lived his life, managed his large farm, played cricket and died in a country where the vast majority were black and poor, there is not a single mention of black life or black people. They are simply rendered invisible, non-existent, not having the cricketing 'blood' of the ruling white race.

The ugly notion of 'blood' as the determinant of national identity is a racist, exclusionary concept known viscerally by black men and women of sport the world over. Jack Johnson knew it, as did Muhammad Ali. So did Jesse Owens, Basil D'Oliveira of Cape Town and entire generations of black American baseball players who were driven from the professional game by its racist controllers and forced into a Jim Crow league structure. Pioneers such as Fleet Walker, the first black professional to play in a major baseball league (in 1884), were hounded out after half a decade. Walker's biographer,

David W. Zang, summarised the importance given to issues of 'blood' by race theorists and 'scientists' in the lifetimes of these early black players:

> *The idea of distinct racial heredity held sway during most of Fleet Walker's lifetime. While elsewhere in North America a person's social standing and racial identity depended on a number of factors, including skin colour, anatomical features and hair texture, in the United States blood was perceived as the vital source of race distinction. The belief that blood contained the seeds of differing traits between the races was an attractive one for race theorists because it grounded race distinctions in an immutable biological fact.[3]*

## Zoning in on schools

Henderson's article regenerated the same fallacies of 'blood' within the heart of English cricket, while, on the educational front, three other related issues converged during that July. Firstly, a survey conducted by researchers from Newcastle and Hertfordshire universities concluded that primary school children (now becoming thoroughly institutionalised within the cultural and learning tramlines of the first two Key Stages of the National Curriculum), 'are in danger of developing a narrow view of national culture which could lead to racist attitudes'.[4] The survey's results showed white children to be 'confused about whether black people were British', and the researchers themselves were concerned about the 'number of children whose responses indicated a potential for racism'. During the same week that the survey was released, Dr Nick Tate, the chief executive of the School Curriculum and Assessment Authority, made a nationally publicised speech to a group of Shropshire headteachers. In it, he pronounced that 'minority cultures could only flourish' if there were 'a majority culture which is sure of itself' that helps British children 'feel that they belong to a community which stretches back into the past and forwards into the future, which is so important in giving people a sense of meaning in a world which is in a state of constant social, economic and technological flux.'[5]

Here was one of the most influential figures of the British educational establishment speaking, a policy and institution builder at the centre of the hegemonic National Curriculum and its attendant bodies – and his words provoked a quick response from some black journalists. Writing in the *Times Educational Supplement*, Rifat Malik recalled her own past school experiences and being addressed as a 'WOG' (kindly explained as a 'Western Oriental Gentleman' by her teacher). She wondered if, in the context of 'the death of Joy Gardner, the racial stereotyping of crime by Metropolitan Police Commissioner Paul Condon, as well as the demonisation of Islam', there was any change at all in British society's racism: 'Any more of an exalted status for British culture must strike fear into the hearts of black and Asian parents,' she wrote.[6]

If Tate's purpose in making his speech was, as he claimed, 'to stimulate debate' (the same reason given by the editor of *Wisden Cricket Monthly* for publishing Henderson's article), he certainly persuaded the imperial nostalgia-wallahs to break cover and appear in the open on the letters' pages of the *Daily Mail*. One correspondent, who claimed to be a nursery teacher, rejected any notion of bringing the experiences and knowledge of Britain's black communities into the classroom. Under the headline, 'We've lost our grip on greatness', he professed:

> *Of course we should be teaching children what it means to be British, and the sensible words of Dr Tate are long overdue. When setting up our school we were told to buy a black dolly and puzzles which represented children of other cultures, and it was suggested that we might like to serve rice and other foreign food at break time to reflect the multicultural environment around us.*
>
> *Let's make a stand for Britain and preserve what rich heritage, culture and traditions we have before it's too late.[7]*

These sentiments were reinforced by the testimony of another letter-writer looking back to a time when 'a quarter of the world map was still pink and though we watched various countries casting off the colonial cloak, we felt like the Father of the Nations, sending them out, fully clothed, into a maturing world'. Tate's words seemed to have evoked intimations of a remembered divine paternalism that yearned to be reborn: 'God-like, we bestrode the other cultures of the world, a young British white male, growing up then, could truly feel he had "won first prize in the lottery of life". No wonder people are searching for some essential "Britishness" to teach our children'.[8]

Hard on the heels of Tate's speech came a statement by prime minister Major on his 'sporting vision' for schools. In a widely-publicised promise of a sporting renaissance for young people in Britain, Major (a cricket enthusiast often photographed holding a bat, or sipping tea at test matches on the pavilion balcony) gave little indication of any extra resources for the development of sport within inner-city communities and their predominantly black young people.[9] Instead, he advocated that National Lottery money be spent to establish a number of elite sporting academies, reinforcing the model of sport as under the command of establishment bodies with the power to exclude, by culture and habit, the young people of the struggling urban neighbourhoods of Britain. As A. Sivanandan commented on the cricket authorities running the English game who control the academies and training institutions of the sport: 'They are the last stand of Empire. In football, by and large, it's the fans that are racist, but in cricket, it's the establishment. It's *institutionalised* racism. The smell of imperialism is in your nostrils all the time.'[10] Such authorities would become further empowered through the Major initiative, and the hierarchies of British sporting culture further consolidated.

## The banner and the bell

During the summer of 1995, the West Indies cricket team toured England and played six test matches. Yet the English cricket authorities were grim hosts. In all the test match grounds from Leeds to Lord's, from Manchester, Birmingham and Nottingham to the Oval in south London, bans were introduced on the activities of British-based Caribbean supporters who in previous test match series between the teams had created so much extra excitement and verve, and given the West Indies players the feeling that they were playing in front of their own people. As Emma Lindsey, writing in the *Observer*, put it: 'Long days of banners, horns, call and response and drumming are over. Officialdom has seen to that with the banning of flags and drums for the entire Cornhill test series.'[11] Thus the British cricket establishment and its watchdogs were attacking expressions of the enthusiasm, loyalty and wit of the Caribbean people in England, the music from the terraces and the punning and wordplay on huge white sheets that satirised the vestiges of empire and arrogance, the sheer joy of being alive in live cricket. It was a group of Caribbean supporters who dubbed the 1984 victory of the West Indies in winning every match a 'Blackwash', by writing the word on a fluttering home-made banner on the final day of the Oval test. Since Lord Beginner's *Victory Test Match* celebration calypso which followed the Lord's test in 1950, the cultural affirmation of rising nationhood on the terraces had always been most strongly carried in music and the sounds of horn and drum. Now, in 1995, there was close to silence from the depleting ranks of West Indies supporters, and, although the occasional forbidden banner of encouragement ('Lash dem Lara!') rose up from the whitening terraces, the new 'culture' was being provided by England fans wearing glitzy wigs, party hats and Elvis Presley costumes and masks, replacing the vibrant cricket culture of Caribbean people and overlaying it with a commercial alternative. Here, one might feel, were the echoes of the silence demanded of Caribbean drumming by the colonial plantocracy during the centuries of slavery.

Now at the Oval, private security firms, their officers carrying walkie-talkie radios and wearing fluorescent yellow bibs, patrolled the crowd, searching out the 'offensive' sounds and symbols of the Caribbean. One West Indies woman supporter was reported to have been denied entry to the ground until she surrendered a nine-inch staff bearing a Caribbean flag[12]. Meanwhile, test match admission prices soared, with space for public seating more and more being converted to corporate hospitality boxes for firms entertaining their clients and socialites wanting to be 'seen' as a part of the cricketing aristocracy. And the attempts to sabotage the effectiveness of the West Indies' fast bowlers on the field, by the imposition of restrictions against short-pitched bowling against England batsmen, resonated with the restrictions on their supporters' exuberant efforts to inspire and goad their players from the midst of the crowd. As one Barbadian fan commented during the Manchester test match: 'The noise is part of cricket and supporting your team. It's going to be detrimental to the West Indian team not to have that. There's hardly any of us here and because we're not all sitting together the players can't see or hear us.'[13]

Yet Caribbean supporters, not to be silenced or made invisible, found free vantage points on scaffolding, roofs and apartment blocks outside the ground, and blew conches, drummed and shouted their encouragement over the brick walls of the Oval. And as the West Indies team drummed up a massive 692 in the first innings, the television coverage flashed to a black man in the crowd, standing up and clanging a large school bell. A white spectator from another part of the crowd answered him, blowing furiously down the horn of a shell. All the while, Lara and Richie Richardson of Antigua flayed the England bowling to all parts of the boundary during a stand of 188 runs.

This pile-up of clampdowns upon black cricket caused insult and disappointment during a month when young black people were being re-labelled by the Metropolitan Police as the prime cause of London street crime, and were being harassed and humiliated in ever greater numbers as a result of the hi-tech 'Operation Eagle Eye'. So much so that, during the July/August 1995 period, three times the usual number of complaints about police behaviour were reported to black community monitoring organisations in Greenwich and Newham. This in a context where black young men were already ten times more likely to be stopped and searched than their white counterparts.[14] Yet the cricket abuses, like the menacing activities of the police, provoked protest and counter-organisation. Not only did black cricketers themselves angrily respond to Henderson's article on television, in letter columns and through the courts, but progressive journalists and cricket supporters responded with public meetings and the formation of an embryonic national campaign, 'Hit Racism for Six'. As founder Mike Marqusee, author of a seminal book on English cricket and national decline, *Anyone But England*,[15] declared at the organisation's launching the day before the final test match at the Oval: 'We want to ensure that all cricket lovers can enjoy the game without fear of harassment or abuse. We want to ensure that cricket is not used to promote racist or xenophobic ideas.'[16]

## Exclusion and non-selection

The continuing debate around the non-selection of black players for the England team has frequently focused upon Devon Malcolm, who, despite his match-winning performances, has consistently been left out of the national team – only to be brought back for what team supremo and selector Ray Illingworth has called 'one-off' appearances, particularly at the

Oval, where the hard wicket has often enhanced Malcolm's bounce and speed. By August 1995, ex-England opening batsman and TV cricketing sage Geoff Boycott was amazed to see how the selectors had put the fastest bowler in the world 'on the scrapheap'. 'There are occasions when I feel like the most frustrated cricketer in the country,'[17] Malcolm has declared in response to the in-out attitude to him by the selectors, and his frustration came to the boil in June 1994 when he was included in the thirteen-player squad for the Lord's test match against New Zealand, then excluded the day before the match began. 'Why the hell did they pick me if they weren't going to play me?' asked Malcolm.[18] Many thousands more cricket supporters posed the same question when he was left out for four matches after playing in just the one domestic test following his phenomenal performance against the South Africans in August 1994. Of that onslaught, the South African pace bowler, Allan Donald, who saw Malcolm bowl at the closest of quarters and who, alongside Malcolm, is reckoned to be among the fastest, observed: 'England would be stupid to ignore Devon Malcolm. His pace last year was unbelievable. He moved the ball away and I've never seen anyone bowl so fast and put it in the right place.'[19]

Yet Malcolm's occasional press-quoted dissatisfaction about this whimsical and unreasonable treatment by the selectors (referred to euphemistically in the *Guardian* as 'the uneven contours of his England career') was considered 'not cricket' by the England cricket establishment and its spokesmen.[20] Considering the merits or otherwise of Malcolm's recall to the England team for the final test in August 1995, the *Daily Mail* cricket correspondent, Peter Johnson, wrote that 'the only obstacle to his return was probably his loud and persistent insistence on it'.[21] For, whatever else, black players must keep quiet, wait, stay obedient on the cricket plantation and be grateful for the gift of selection; must never question the wisdom or selection processes of the overseers of the cricket establishment who hold players' futures in the selections they make.

This truth became more blatantly apparent during the England winter tour of South Africa (1995/6). Cricket in South Africa, as with all aspects of life, has been an area of anti-racist struggle throughout its history. Yet this first tour since the formal end of apartheid showed that, while in South African urban areas there are moves towards genuine development and progress for black South African cricketers, the England touring squad had not shown a similar process of development. Again, the issue centred around the treatment of Malcolm.

It was almost as if he were being willed to fail, every obstacle was being placed in his way, as if a black cricketer, even one with over 100 test match wickets behind him, must be convinced that he can never finally win through. For Malcolm, only recently recovered from keyhole surgery on his knee, was yanked out of the first-class match in which he was playing in Soweto – where he had been publicly and warmly congratulated by president Nelson Mandela as a role model for South Africa's township youth[22] - and taken to Pretoria for a concentrated 'coaching session' by bowling coach Peter Lever, in an effort to change his bowling action. All this crude and humiliating restructure did was to disorient his bowling rhythm and put more pain upon his injured knee. Following this training debacle, Lever announced: 'He has pace and fitness, but that is all. The rest of his cricket is a nonentity.'[23] Illingworth followed this up at a press conference by saying that Malcolm had 'no cricketing brain'.[24] He further declared: 'It's not worked out with Devon as we hoped... we have not had the time to do the two months' work we wanted with him... at the moment he would not frighten you [the press] never mind the South African batsmen.'[25]

These comments came two weeks after Malcolm's victory in the High Court and the awarding of damages to him for the racist statements made about him in *Wisden Cricket Monthly*, on whose editorial board sits the England captain, Mike Atherton. Another member of the board, sports journalist Frank Keating, wrote angrily in the *Guardian* about the events in South Africa. Under the headline 'Devon mugged by crudely wielded Lever', he wrote: 'Malcolm, as the only black man in England's team, has by all accounts wholeheartedly leapt to the battle standard of Mandela's new nation. I agree it would be grotesque to think the England management has treated its black man as an olde tyme Afrikaner of legend, but I cannot remember ever reading any sports page and being so angry.'[26] The 'patronising disdain' and 'brutish affront' to Malcolm, as Keating put it, were condemned by other sports writers of the establishment press. Ian Botham wrote that the bowler was being treated like a 'drinks waiter',[27] and Simon Barnes in *The Times* observed how Malcolm was being used as 'the Aunt Sally of the half-baked. In the summer he was the principal butt of that grubby piece of racism in the magazine *Wisden Cricket Monthly*. And now the England management has made a vast public meal of the fact that Malcolm hasn't re-modelled his bowling action at their behest.'[28] Even the conservative London *Evening Standard* described Illingworth as the 'Obersturmbannfuhrer who has publicly humiliated Devon Malcolm', at the side of a cartoon showing the manager in Gestapo gear,[29] and Donald Trelford, ex-editor of the *Observer* and now writing in the *Daily Telegraph*, wrote of 'the lofty and doubtless unwitting colonial touch of the England management. I was reminded of the exasperated way the old white settlers in Kenya and former Rhodesia used to talk about the Africans: "Lazy lot, can't teach them anything, you know."'[30]

Kim Barnett, ex-captain of Derbyshire, who nourished and supported Malcolm's bowling over many years, described the 'slur' on his team-mate: 'Illingworth and Lever seem to be taking turns to belittle him. The South Africans must be laughing their socks off.'[31] Not black and progressive South Africans though. They would quickly recognise a new import of English-brand apartheid behaviour very close in its essence to the system which they struggled against for decades. That is also the nature of Devon Malcolm's struggle and that of all black British cricketers who have international aspirations. For Malcolm was not picked for that first test match at Pretoria, performed well with six wickets in the second at Johannesburg, only to be discarded again in the two that followed.[32] What was again clear from this encounter between South Africa and England was that black cricketers of both countries still have formidable barriers to break down at the very crux of the sport they love – obstructions that are symbolic of all other walls of racism in the societies where they live.

## Malcolm's inspiration

It was on such an uneven cricketing landscape, brought down to the very local level, that a team of schoolboy cricketers travelled up from Sheffield in South Yorkshire in July 1995, to play in the finals of the *Yorkshire Post* under-13 competition at their county ground and test match arena, Headingley in Leeds.

The next day, when the *Yorkshire Post* printed a match report and a full scorecard, from numbers one to eleven in the batting order, readers could see that all the names were Islamic.[33] Nine of these boys had their family origins in the Mirpur region of southern Kashmir, now Pakistan. Another's parents were from Sylhet in Bangladesh, and Yahya Ahmed, an arrivant two years before from Sana'a, Yemen, was most likely the first ever person from that country to have played cricket at any international venue in Britain.

These boys were all students at Earl Marshal Comprehensive School in the inner city of north-east Sheffield, and all regular members of the Devon Malcolm Cricket Centre which, since 1990, had been an integral part of the interaction between the school and its local community of Pakistani, Caribbean, Yemeni, Somali and white South Yorkshire families. Malcolm himself, originally from Jamaica, had arrived in Sheffield as a teenager, played for local Caribbean, Asian and regional league sides before finding success and fame for Derbyshire and England. The Centre's coach is another Jamaican Englishman, Steve Taylor, ex-opening bowler partner of Malcolm in their younger days of South Yorkshire league cricket and Derbyshire Seconds. Taylor's son, Bjorn (named after the Swedish tennis ace), is also a fine young cricketer and regular member of the Centre's team. Of the three other joint founders, two are Mike Atkins and Owen Gittens, Barbadian veterans of Sheffield's Caribbean community organisation and cricket club. They remember boyhood matches between the canefields with other youths named Sobers, Hall and Griffith. The other is the school's former headteacher, a man of Essex who grew up bowling seamers on its green and dewy pitches, and who played for England schools in the early 1960s.

The Centre arose through a sustaining love of cricket manifested by Caribbean and Pakistani communities in inner-city Sheffield, and the local school's commitment to respond to this enthusiasm. It was nursed and grew in vibrancy in a context where Yorkshire County Cricket Club and its official structures have shown no interest at all in the county's young cricketers from black and arrivant communities. Injustice and rejection willed the Centre on, gave it a particular aim and aspiration – to produce the county's first black representative cricketers, to darken the white rose and make it the emblem of all Yorkshire, not just white Yorkshire.

It was to this pioneering centre that Malcolm donated a proportion of the damages he gained from *Wisden Cricket Monthly* for the publication of

Henderson's racist article. As Ross Slater, a journalist on the *Caribbean Times*, wrote under the headline, 'Sweet dreams are made of this: youth to benefit from the dismissal of cricket's racists': 'The school children at the Centre have their own battle to face against cricket's established racist attitudes. Based in the heart of South Yorkshire, the youngsters know all too well that the County Cricket Club have never had a black native of Yorkshire on their staff. How heart-warming that money from *Wisden Cricket Monthly*, the guardian of conservatism in cricket, will now help them to realise their dream!'[34]

Here's how one of the first budding players from the Centre, Nasar Mohammed, expressed his sense of loss and deflected self-blame at being excluded from the possibility of playing for his homeplace county in the days before Sachin Tendulkar, the young Indian prodigy, became the first black player to take the field for Yorkshire – when the county had to go thousands of miles to find such a pathfinder while hundreds play in parks and on grounds in the cities scattered across it:

> *Unfortunately for me, I was born in Pakistan and my family moved from Rawalpindi and migrated to Britain where we moved to Yorkshire, to Sheffield, when I was at the tender age of four years and three months.*
>
> *I use the word 'unfortunate' because being born in Pakistan automatically ruled out the possibility of me representing my home and beloved county of Yorkshire as a cricketer. However, I did not realise this until I was thirteen years old. Up until that age I had my eyes set on the white rose of my county. When I realised that I would not be able to play for Yorkshire, I felt for the first time in my life locked up in a prison, and outside the prison walls people were playing cricket for a purpose. My own crime was being an 'overseas-born player', as they said.*
>
> *'Why can't I play for Yorkshire?' I asked. 'I'm just as much Yorkshire bred as they are.'*
>
> *Meanwhile I did not let these things bother me and I played as much cricket as I could. I played with Frecheville, a local club, and also in the Asian league.*[35]

This is not the testimony of a cricketer who is rejecting either his new county or his new country which have nurtured his game. His words are those of a young man expressing a deep sense of unfairness, disappointment and exclusion caused by those who organise and play cricket in his place in the world, the place he shares with them. 'You are here but you do not belong here,' they tell him. 'You are here but you cannot be with us, you cannot be one of us. You are a foreigner and not a part of us.'

Thus, when the project of the cricket centre developed in his community, Nasar seized upon it as a new, welcoming opportunity. 'I went to all the meetings which I was able to attend and also the cricket sessions run by Steve Taylor,' he recalls. When the Pakistani cricket captain, the legendary Imran Khan, visited the Centre in December 1990, Nasar's sense of loss was transformed into an intense cultural prize, particularly when he was chosen to face the great all-rounder as he bowled the ceremonial first ball in the Centre's nets: 'I was sweating and my throat was dry. There were about 700 people watching me and Imran Khan, and once he had let that ball go from his hands, I felt that all eyes were on me. The ball was a full toss, so to show a bit of respect I played a forward defensive stroke. After the nets, me and Imran had many photos taken together.'

There is much to be learned from Nasar's story. It shows us how rejection provokes self-doubt and a loss of confidence in young cricketers. But it shows too how it breeds a search for alternatives – in a cricketing sense creating your own all-Asian teams and leagues and where you can strive to play without rejection or racism. It shows, too, how such vices also bring forward struggle; a fighting campaign in cricket for inclusion, for equal treatment, for sporting and thus social justice, for an end to racism in all dimensions of life, in sport and culture as well as in politics and economics. It is that very resistance to the paradigm of race in sport, not the smokescreen of 'national identity' invoked by Henderson, that is the true issue, the reality that counts to young cricketers growing up and learning their game in the inner cities.

'Why is cricket important to you?' I asked this question of some of the young players at the Devon Malcolm Cricket Centre. 'Cricket makes me feel proud,' declared Tahir, one young Pakistani all-rounder. 'Cricket has built up my courage by letting me play some matches when, even if we are losing, never to lose hope and to teach us that there is always a chance.' And writing his thoughts down, he broke into poetry:

> *When I bat and bowl*
> *I remember the courage I had lost,*
> *And what cricket had brought back.*

Hope and courage, qualities of cricket, but needed for much more too in the British inner city. And for Imran Ali that other is ambition: 'Cricket is important because if I become a cricketer my Mum and Dad will say "My son has become a cricketer" and I'll become quite famous. And the Pakistani community will get happy and say, "Here comes another Imran Khan!"' Yet Imran's models are Imran, of course, but also 'Gooch, Ambrose and my brother Nasar', with his favourite player Darren Gough of Barnsley and his 'second favourite player' Waqar Younis. So there is no simple or one-dimensional nationalism here, no scope for the narrow responses of 'cricket tests', 'blood' tests of national identity or anything so facile or close to the processes of quasi-fascism. The truth is that the young Imran, like most developing inner-city cricketers from the arrivant communities, is immensely and sophisticatedly cosmopolitan about his tastes and loyalties in cricket. They are young sporting internationalists who set aside all boundaries of nation and race, and that is part of their new vitality and vision, forever beyond the sights of Henderson, Tebbit and their confreres. Imran writes, for example, of the Jamaican teacher who has taught him the game with so much love, dedication and skill: 'Mr Taylor is a great teacher at Earl Marshal and he learned me how to bowl and to bat. He learns you properly, he gets everything into your mind before you start. He is a brilliant teacher. When I become older and become a cricketer, I will always remember him.'

Nothing is as dangerously simplistic as Henderson's assertions about a single-track national identity, and nothing so unreal in the context of inner-city cricket. These young cricketers move with ease every day between languages – be they Punjabi, Urdu, Arabic, Somali, the varieties of Caribbean Creole as well as South Yorkshire English – they cross cultures, religions and the frontiers of sport. Their bats are made in Pakistan and signed by Imran, their bowling machine is named 'Devon' and their pads and gloves are manufactured in Nottingham, London and India when their fathers can afford to buy them. Zahid supports Lancashire although he lives in Yorkshire. This is not apostasy but merely the result of staying with his uncle in Manchester when he first came to live in England. He also supports Pakistan, and why not? He is an internationalist like his friends, and not bound to the absolute rules and sentiments of nations and boundaries. His favourite cricketer is Robin Smith, a transplanted white South African. Mohsin too proclaims, 'Cricket for me represents my country, Pakistan', but then he writes of a greater and wider polity expressed through his cricket team and its Centre: 'Keep on trying together and we'll keep on winning.' The word is 'together', nations and youth playing, organising, cooperating, living in loyalty together in the village at the heart of their British city, in Yorkshire.

For Yahya, the cricketer from the Yemen, and also for his two Somali friends on the point of breaking into the team, cricket was unheard of until he crossed over land and sea to Sheffield in 1993. He made some Pakistani friends while studying in his 'English as a second language' class. Among them was Sarfraz Nawaz, who scored a fifty at Headingley in the *Yorkshire Post* competition, described in the match report as 'fluent' and full of fine and powerful drives. So to meet young Pakistanis in Firvale, Sheffield, is also to meet cricket, and Yahya held bat and ball with his new friends, discovering a game which, in the Arabian highlands of his birthplace, was not even a whisper in the searing sun. At first, he remembers, his Pakistani classmates laughed at him. 'I had trouble batting the ball properly and bowling. But I said to myself, I can do it, my body can do anything I want it to. The power is not only in the muscle, it is in the brain.' So Yahya achieved talent and style with his Jamaican coach and cover drives of grace and excellence.

Thinking of Yahya, of Imran, Sarfraz and Mohsin, of Rob Miah from Bangladesh with his wicket keeper's pads and the careful tutoring of Steve Taylor, what could be so limiting, so anachronistic and future-crushing as the crude application of the bigoted cliches and mindset of 'national identity'? Here is an organic and working internationalism with cricket as its nucleus and catalyst, fomenting unity and energy between young people of scattered, diverse and divided communities. It is what cricket is for. Young people are making new identities for themselves in the context of the world culture they represent, developing in their schools, their streets, their playgrounds and their cricket centre. They are the creators of a new concept of 'England', forging new versions of selfhood in the old 'steel city', as in urban contexts through the country. Their raw and often prodigious cricketing talent, if developed and canalised with skills and commitment like those of Steve Taylor, could create a team of world beaters. For the new English cricket power is not coming from the public school playing fields or suburban parks, or from the echoing greens of the traditional 'English game with the beautiful name'. It is coming direct from between the traffic, terrace houses and blocks of Bradford and the London boroughs, from Sheffield, Manchester and Nottingham, from smaller and less fashionable northern cities like Dewsbury and Oldham, Rotherham and Huddersfield. The new urban cricketer is not a young person of bigoted or narrow nationalism. His friends are from families that have moved across continents and migrated over oceans. A Yemeni boy declares:

> *I crossed the seas*
> *I travelled thousands of miles*
> *I watched the stars and the moon*

and now he has come to Sheffield and he plays cricket.

The Pakistani boy writes of the old game of Empire, now transformed by great players like Richards and Imran, Gavaskar, Lara and Warne, Waqar and Hadlee – but also by young cricketers like himself. This is from a poem by Farooq:

> *It is a sport which has its own passion*
> *Has its own pace,*
> *For me has its own skill*
> *But most of all has its own identity.*
> *I am a young Pakistani lad*
> *Who loves cracking the ball over the boundary*
> *Who loves to smash the stumps*
> *As fast and skilfully as Waqar Younis –*
> *Cricket will always stay the best sport for me!*

Here is a world in a sport, neither a mere nation nor a group of 'blood', a world and its people at play in urban streets, finding pride, confidence, power and a new friendship of equals together in a striving to cooperate and win through in their lives. It is the cricket of the future.

## REFERENCES

[1] Robert Henderson, 'Is it in the blood?', *Wisden Cricket Monthly* (July 1995)

[2] Dudley Nourse, *Cricket in the Blood* (London, Hodder and Stoughton, 1949)

[3] David W. Zang, *Fleet Walker's Divided Heart* (Nebraska, University of Nebraska Press, 1995)

[4] See article by Diane Hofkins in the *Times Educational Supplement* (21 July 1995)

[5] *Times Educational Supplement* (21 July 1995)

[6] *Times Educational Supplement* (28 July 1995)

[7] *Daily Mail* (21 July 1995)

[8] This and the preceeding quote are from ibid.

[9] *Observer* (23 July 1995)

[10] See article by Rob Steen in *Sunday Times* (30 July 1995)

[11] *Observer* (30 July 1995)

[12] See article by Eddie Butler in *Observer* (27 August 1995)

[13] *Observer* (30 July 1995)

[14] See article by Eleanor Mills in *Observer* (27 August 1995)

[15] Mike Marqusee, *Anyone But England* (London, Verso, 1994)

[16] *Morning Star* (24 August 1995) and Mike Marqusee, 'Hit Racism for Six', *CARF* (No.27, August/September 1995)

[17] See article by David Foot in *Guardian* (22 August 1995)

[18] *Sun* (16 June 1994)

[19] *Today* (19 August 1995)

[20] *Guardian* (22 August 1995)

[21] *Daily Mail* (21 August 1995)

[22] Mandela addressed Malcolm during an interval in the match: 'I know you. You are the destroyer. You don't know how much you have done for cricket and sport and people in South Africa.' *The Cricketer* (December 1995); *Daily Express* (15 January 1996)

[23] *Guardian* (31 October 1995)

[24] *Daily Express* (17 January 1996)

[25] *Guardian* (31 October 1995)

[26] *Guardian* (2 November 1995)

[27] *Daily Express* (17 January 1996)

[28] *The Times* (1 November 1995)

[29] *Evening Standard* (2 November 1995)

[30] *Daily Telegraph* (2 November 1995)

[31] *Star*, Sheffield (1 November 1995)

[32] When Malcolm was finally picked up again for the last match of the series, which South Africa easily won, Illingworth blamed him directly for the defeat - finger-wagging him and telling him he was 'crap' in the dressing room, in front of his white team-mates (see *Daily Express* (18 January 1996)) And when Malcolm, on his return to England, questioned whether he might have been treated differently if he were a white cricketer, he was told by the Test and County Cricket Board that his words were offensive and that he could face a £10, 000 disciplinary fine.

[33] *Yorkshire Post* (15 July 1995)

[34] *Caribbean Times* (4 November 1995)

[35] See article by Nasar Mohammed in *Plus 16* (Sheffield, 1991)

# 5.

# THE ECHOING STREET
## Reinventing Cricket
## (1996)

*The Sun does arise*
*And make happy the skies;*
*The merry bells ring*
*To welcome the Spring;*
*The skylark and thrush,*
*The birds of the bush,*
*Sing louder around*
*To the bells' chearful sound,*
*While our sports shall be seen*
*On the ecchoing Green.*[1]

THE HISTORY OF CRICKET IN ENGLAND shows it to have emerged from country villages and green suburbs. That is its origin and its idyll. Yet its modern contradiction is that the game's most vibrant future is in the hearts of our cities, in the streets, car parks and waste ground of our most neglected and violated urban areas.

When William Blake wrote *The Ecchoing Green* as part of his 'Songs of Innocence' in 1789, he heard beyond the 'chearful sound' of cricketing voices 'under the oaks' and with his prophetic eyes also saw the sun setting on the 'darkening green'. For during that year he wrote also of events in France, of insurgent Parisians raising their 'darken'd limbs out of the caves of night', of the 'morning star arising above the black waves', of urban oppression.

For cricket, this mythical and pastoral game so associated with the continuity and stability of the eternal mainstream of England outside the walls of the inner cities, has for over a century been accepted as the emblem of what is pure and uncorrupted in English life, both at home and 'in the colonies'. Indeed, anything else simply wasn't and isn't cricket. Yet what had been accepted as symbolic and typical of the English ethos was, and still is, institutionally often fiercely hostile to new contributions and accretions, particularly if these are viewed by its ruling elite as too urban and close to working people – or 'foreign' and coming from cultures and individuals who are not 'one of us'.

This is why, within the multiplicity of club structures and cricket leagues across the country, 'two crickets' exist in England now (a point made with dramatic clarity in Caryl Phillips' play, *Playing Away*), and why so many black cricketers opt for the security of their own leagues where the exclusiveness and associated racism of the white structures become much less of a regular weekend issue. The 'Gentlemen and Players' dichotomy and snobbery that plagued the sport for decades has now taken on a new identity: it is the suburbs/inner city duality that now casts the most fundamental division within the sport – most often expressed through the realities of culture and race, and it is poisoning the opportunities for the integrity of British cricket as well as causing the institutional neglect of thousands of very talented, enthusiastic and mostly black young inner city cricketers. It also drives thousands of potential spectators away from watching the sport they love, denying them the right to express their cultures at test match stadiums – where officious stewards refuse entry, take their drums, flags, horns or conches and expel them from the ground if they dare to make 'un-English' sounds.

Partly as a consequence of this policy and practice of exclusion manifested at almost every level in the game, in those inner city neighbourhoods of Yorkshire, Lancashire, London and the Midlands, we are seeing the virtual reinvention of cricket – this time as an urban game. Cricketers have not traditionally been products of the inner city, and those who have achieved major representative success have often made it against the odds. Although there have been some outstanding exceptions – one of the most prominent in the post-war period being Graham Gooch from Leyton, East London – John Arlott's *100 Greatest Batsmen*, for example, reveals only one instance (Patsy Hendren) who was inner city bred, and even those great professionals who played for the London 'urban counties' like Surrey's Jack Hobbs (from Cambridgeshire) or Alec Bedser (from Reading), or Middlesex's Denis Compton (from Hendon) came from the suburbs or a rural county beyond. My own experience as a young 'hopeful' in Essex, playing in the early sixties for junior representative teams, soon told me that there was little opportunity for young talent from the inner city boroughs. The main youth elevens which fed through into the county first and second teams were the young professionals of the 'Club and Ground' and the favourites of the 'Young Amateurs' squad, composed mainly of public schoolboys with the occasional grammar school product included. Thus when these two young sides played against each other it created a definite clash of cricketing cultures akin to the 'Gentlemen vs. Players' confrontation. Looking back at old scorecards of 'Young Amateurs' matches – which included the school of the batsman after his name on the batting order, my own 'Hornchurch Grammar School' picked itself out against the prestigious public schools of Tonbridge, Brentwood, Newport and Repton. There was never an urban school in sight – even suburban grammar schools like mine were not really considered as the nurseries of young cricketers and I was certainly seen as something of a social oddity by some of my public school team-mates. Who of them had heard of my nondescript 'modern' school, established in the fifties in an unremarkable London suburb?

Now the streets of England's inner cities echo with the sounds of bat, ball and multilingual voices. Where the new communities have arrived, so has their cricket. Ironically, they have brought it with them, their own anti-colonial versions from Kashmir, Barbados, Punjab, Guyana or Lahore – versions freely adapted not from models in London or Bradford, but from a game developed in their countries of origin, learned applied and emulated from imperial occupiers. Despite the notion of cricket being the *English* summer game, it has only convincingly arrived in the inner cities with the ways of these communities – in particular from the Caribbean, Pakistan and India. To claim that these peoples have 'reinvented' the game in a new, urban and internationalist context that is far from English exclusiveness and xenophobia is not far-fetched. A sport takes on characteristics according to the conditions wherein it is played and the culture of those who play it.

Sometimes culture is translated as 'temperament' by shallow and hostile commentators and vicious myths, attached to race, develop around invented characteristics: the notion of the 'fiery' and 'petulant' Pakistani who is assumed to be this way because he is a Moslem: or the 'aggressive' or 'casual' West Indian who once he is down he is out. These fictions have frequently been the curse of cricket, created often by the narrow attitudes and ignorance of those who write in the national and local press and claim to be its pundits. And they spread right through the game, down to local clubs and leagues. When I was a boy I grew up with the assumption being put to me from the heart of the English game that West Indian batsmen were only 'sloggers' with superhuman and instinctive powers to hit almost everything as far as they could. Yet it wasn't until I worked in the Caribbean and observed in Guyana – a goldmine of some of the finest Caribbean batsmen, and saw how young players *had* to play straight and build hard defences in Guyanese countryside. Contact with a wild swipe would mean a lost ball and close of play when you were practising on narrow paths and clearings between bush and marsh.

In city streets and playgrounds across England cricket is shaped by this combination of environment and tradition – and a certain spirit of resistance, a dimension of the extra will and struggle needed to tackle the racism and exclusion inhabiting the English game. Young Pakistani cricketers in Sheffield, for example, while they are struggling for skill know they are also struggling against racist obstacles in the game which have stopped even their most talented young cricketers moving towards playing for Yorkshire. And there are less insidious features of the sport too. The popularity of wrist spin among the same schoolboys and youths is not only due to the traditions of some brilliant Pakistani spinners – from Abdul Qadir to Mushtaq. It is also due to sheer improvisation in physical situations where attempts to follow Waqar and Wasim may be restricted by a shortage of space for run-ups. In such situations creativity is all, and new ideas and strategies flourish. Like Blake and his urban inventiveness and originality, so these young cricketers grow according to what they can achieve within their streets, pushing their boundaries backwards and finding new space, techniques and insights. Just like the great poet himself, who declared of his poetry: 'My streets are my ideas of imagination.'

Race and class have become as central to cricket as bat and ball. This truth is manifested every summer day in Yorkshire cities as the talent of young black cricketers remains institutionally undeveloped and their skills given little opportunity to achieve in representative cricket at the county level. With all the excellence among young Asian cricketers in Bradford, Sheffield, Leeds and the smaller cities, still no black cricketer resident in Yorkshire has played for the county team. The adopted Sheffielder born in Jamaica – Devon Malcolm, who has captured over a century of Test Match wickets for England, could not play for the county despite living, studying and playing in Sheffield, and had to switch counties to find a professional career for Derbyshire. Even with the new dispensation that allows non-Yorkshire born players to play for the county, still no local black cricketer has been selected – despite the club officials foraging the world to find overseas players like the Indian Sachin Tendulkar and the Antiguan Richie Richardson to help lift them from lowly positions in the County Championship table. If only they looked to their own inner cities, where they would find talent in abundance! Other counties like Derbyshire, Lancashire and Essex have done better, but the power of young cricket in inner city neighbourhoods still stays virtually untapped. It could certainly do much to advance the fortunes of the national side —at present practically lilywhite, if it were properly recognised, coached and developed.

Instead, young urban cricketers continue to struggle with poor facilities for the sport which brings them pride, confidence and intellectual as well as physical development. For their cricket is a cricket of the imagination, a pursuit of the creative. There is nothing dull or routine about it. For while playing it they take on racism too, not only from the official bodies which neglect them and leave them out by attitudes and actions of those poisoned by fear and bigotry. A few days ago in Sheffield, some Pakistani and Somali boys were playing with a bat and soft ball in the car park of a working men's club. The club steward, full of racist insults, came storming out flailing at the young cricketers as they harmlessly practised. An everyday occurrence perhaps and many would say not particularly noteworthy – we have all, as boy cricketers, been chased from parks and recreation grounds by angry park keepers zealously guarding flower beds or the windows of their huts. But the difference is in the racism as well as the sheer absence of venues and resources, and such incidents symbolise the exclusion at local, county and national levels that young black inner city cricketers face.

The development of pathfinding urban cricket initiatives such as the Haringey Cricket College and the Devon Malcolm Cricket Centre in north-east Sheffield show crucial ways forward. But how ironic it is and how much a transformation that we can now take cues from the South African government and the strategic ways in which they are building up cricket from the hearts of the townships and urban areas. That planned approach is what we need to emulate in Britain. Not the elite cricket academies which draw young players *away* from their communities, but a concentrated and imaginative initiative in every inner city where cricket flourishes and love of the sport is intense and can be sustained as a source of wider community development and organisation. This will not only support the young 'tygers' of urban cricket, but make the sport's development a genuine catalyst for urban regeneration. Blake would have liked that, as an urban man himself: to make every echoing street resounding with the clip of bat and ball a new 'region of humanity'.

**REFERENCES**

1 William Blake, 'The Ecchoing Green' in *Songs of Innocence* (1789)

# 6.

# DEVON'S MESSAGE
## Nine Blows Against the Old South Africa
## (1996)

ON THE TWENTIETH OF AUGUST 1994, the Jamaican born and Sheffield-bred pace bowler, Devon Malcolm, told a group of mocking white South African international cricketers on a South London cricket pitch: 'You guys are history!'[1]

It was, as it turned out, the penultimate day of the final test match at the Oval cricket ground in Kennington, just up the road from Brixton where thousands of Caribbean migrants had settled in the Fifties and Sixties, and where in 1981 the black youth had confronted and defied the wrath of London's Metropolitan Police.

Malcolm was batting. The first ball from the South African fast bowler Fanie de Villiers had struck him on his helmet, snapping off a piece of its fabric which fell in front of the batsman on the dry and hard turf, provoking contemptuous laughter and invective from the close fielders. Now Devon Malcolm has never been an accomplished batsman. As he walked out to the middle, the television commentator and ex-Australian captain, Richie Benaud, had said with his characteristic understatement, the appearance of Devon with a bat is never 'over-disturbing to the fielding side'. For years his poor eyesight and bespectacled vision made it difficult for him to see the ball clearly. And yet his very unpredictability had thousands of spectators rushing to their seats and agog with expectation whenever he made his slightly nervous stride to the wicket. For Malcolm, now wearing contact lenses, brings out the number eleven in all of us. It is his vulnerability as an essentially honest and unpretentious cricketer that gives him huge popularity among cricket watchers of all races. When he bats anything can happen: he can hit the bowl with all the force of his muscled torso and sinewy arms to any part of the boundary and over it too, as he can just as likely miss the ball with a similarly spectacular power. Whatever he does, thousands in the stands identify with him, step inside his ingenuousness, becoming his batting ordinariness for those few enough moments that he bestrides the pitch. For Devon Malcolm is a common batting cricketer like thousands of others who play on village greens, in parks or *maidans*, recreation grounds, playgrounds or meadows all over the world. He is loved as a common cricketer, ever susceptible, frequently erratic. But he is a common cricketer with a massively uncommon gift and skill. He can bowl as fast as the wind. He can hurl a ball at a batsman with sublime pace and power. His speed is as a Caribbean tempest, ripping palm trees from the fringes of beaches, scattering sheets of galvanised iron from rooftops, pitching fishing boats from their moorings or breaking them across the splintering jetties.

But for now, this was his batting and the ball that struck his helmet was the first of a brief innings. Devon, a mild, well-mannered man, universally liked across the cricket world for his good temper and friendly on-pitch and off-pitch conduct – was enraged. 'You guys are fucking dead!' he exclaimed. Now the team he was playing against represented the southernmost African nation with a huge black majority. It had, through decades of struggle, emerged from a long night of state racism. Its system of apartheid had only very recently been broken and was now being dismantled. Democratic elections had recently put into power the African National Congress government, led by Nelson Mandela. History had been jolted and at last moved forward. In that sense, South Africa's privileged white minority were history. Eleven white men still filled its international team, men who had not shared the privations and struggles of the apartheid years, despite the good intentions and positive attitudes of some of them. Even the opposing England side had three black players. One was Malcolm; the other two, Philip de Freitas and Joey Benjamin, both had diasporan and Caribbean origins and had been England's main wicket takers in South Africa's first innings, Benjamin with 4-43 and de Freitas with 4-93. Yet, despite his success, this was to be Benjamin's only test match and he was to be discarded unreasonably and unfairly as soon as this Oval test match had been completed.

The England first innings soon closed. After his collision with the ball, Devon had the chance to belt one boundary to long on before he made a swift exit at 304 all out. But his anger at De Villiers and the South African fielders who had laughed at him and insulted him when he had been hit, did not recede. During the brief interval between innings, it swelled and strengthened, fusing with his brainpower as it boiled inside him. Apartheid had gone, but this white cricket arrogance had to go along with it. Devon was ready.

His first ball to the opening batsman Gary Kirsten was ferocious, bouncing high and very fast towards his body, forcing the batsman to take evasive action. The television commentator, ex-England batsman David Gower, could already see 'venom' in Malcolm's intent. 'I think Devon means business', he quipped after the hostile opening ball. His third ball reared up again at the batsman's upper body with an untameable pace. Striking the top of the fending Kirsten's bat, the ball popped up for Malcolm to catch as he followed through. A few balls later and the elder Kirsten, Peter, hooked a short and fast leg side Malcolm ball high to the fine leg boundary where de Freitas made a fine and well-judged catch. Hansie Cronje was beaten by sheer speed as he missed an in-cutting well pitched up ball which shattered his stumps. Three down with only one run scored, and all to the rampaging Malcolm. 'Quick as black lightning,' observed Ian Botham, himself as fearless as anyone in the game against fast bowling.

Kepler Wessels, the left-handed South African captain, who had played for Australia during the apartheid years, was next in and next out, as Malcolm changed his angle of delivery, bowling around the wicket and causing Wessel to snick an attempted off drive to wicket keeper Steve Rhodes. 'It's worked!' declared Gower. 'Hmm, very thoughtful bowling,' concluded Geoff Boycott, ex-Yorkshire and England opening batsman who had been clean bowled by Malcolm himself in Devon's early days as a hopeful club cricketer playing for Sheffield United Cricket Club.

Next to be despatched was Brian McMillan, who had been one of Malcolm's prime close-field tormentors when the ball had hit his helmet only an hour or so before. Caught in the slips by Thorpe off a fast offside ball. Then South African wicket-keeper Richardson, LBW from an inswinging full pitched ball. Then Matthews, brilliantly caught by Rhodes jumping to the south London sky to a leg side edge from what Benaud described as 'one of the most fiery deliveries you'll see for a long time'. Fiery, lethal, and seven wickets down, all to Devon Malcolm.

Darren Gough took the eighth, prompting the end of a brave innings by Cullinan for 94: caught again by Thorpe in the slips. But Devon was back again for the ninth – as Jonty Rhodes wafted at a fast, bouncing ball outside the off stump, slashing an edge to the wicket keeper. And the tenth, as last man in Allan Donald was bowled off his pads from another speedy inswinging full-pitched ball. He later wrote, in a tribute to Devon from one great fast bowler to another, 'I have had the honour to have seen one of the most destructive pieces of fast bowling in my cricket career'.[2] And Devon Malcolm had continued and concluded his message. Those 'guys' were history, and Devon had achieved the fourth best bowling ever for England – 9 for 57, with only the great off-spinner Jim Laker having better figures for England in a test match this century.

The impact of Malcolm's destruction of South Africa's residual white test match team had a huge impact as one of the defining moments in twentieth century sport. 'He didn't just bowl out the South Africans that day. He blew them away,'[3] wrote Botham. Here was a black man of the African diaspora, a descendant of African slaves born in Kingston, Jamaica – a Caribbean urban metropolis, symbolically crushing on the field of sport the remnants of the white colonial elite of southern Africa in the heart of the ex-imperial capital city, the very seat of Empire itself, across the Thames from the Houses of Parliament. It was, of course, a powerful event for the black British and those who struggled against the English versions of racism, thousands of whom were residents of south-east London. They had seen racist murders like those of Ruhit Duggal, the youth Rolan Adams in Thamesmead, or John Reid, a white man killed because he had the temerity to marry a woman from Nigeria. They had lived through the establishment of fascist organisations like the British National Party in their part of London, racist marches through the seventies and eighties and the horrendous New Cross fire of 1981, when a fire started by racists had burned to death thirteen young black people at a party.

In April 1993, over a year before Devon's tumult at the Oval, further along the Dover road on the outskirts of south east London in Eltham, a young black man also of Jamaican parentage, Stephen Lawrence, had been stabbed to death by young white racists at a bus stop. His death was later to send convulsions through the British criminal justice system and highlight the curse of England's racism like no other single case in its history. Stephen's parents, Doreen and Neville Lawrence, were to lead a determined and tenacious campaign to uncover the Metropolitan Police's lack of commitment and virtual disengagement from finding Stephen's killers, and to spark the mass public indignation that led to the Macpherson Report of 1999. The Lawrences were also to meet Nelson Mandela and gain his support and solidarity during the South African President's visit to London in May 1993, for news of the death of their son had traversed the world, and found echoes in black communities everywhere.

In October 1995 Devon Malcolm began a tour of South Africa as a member of England's cricket touring party. His selection for the England team between his Oval achievement of August 1994 and the occasion of the South African tour had, as usual, been intermittent and begrudging, but not even the most mean-minded England selection body and management could exclude him from the 1995-6 series in South Africa. This was, of course, England's first tour of the country since the end of South Africa's years of cricket isolation and the end of apartheid. One of the first encounters was a 'friendly' match at Soweto, the first ever cricket match played by a touring side at the huge black suburb outside of Johannesburg's white city. If ever there was a living residue of the apartheid years it was Soweto, and Malcolm's presence in the England team was always going to have a particular pertinence and symbolic power. As the players lined up before the match, a helicopter approached the ground carrying President Nelson Mandela, then at the zenith of his world prestige as South Africa's first post-apartheid head of state and leader of the anti-apartheid movement who had spent 27 years in a prison cell. One by one, he was introduced to the players. On meeting and shaking hands with a proud but abashed Malcolm, he exclaimed, 'Ah, so you are Devon Malcolm, the destroyer!' Clearly it took one to recognise one. Later, the England wicket-keeper, Jack Russell, described the moment: 'When Devon was presented to President Mandela, the look of the two men was something special, only they could fully understand and appreciate the real joy of that moment. I will never forget the smile on Devon's face. He wore it for most of the tour.'[4]

For Malcolm, it was a kind of epiphany: "I felt on top of the world. I was very proud inside to be spoken to like that by President Mandela. I felt that I was involved in the hope of South Africa. So much blood had been shed, so many people had died during the years of apartheid. And I knew my team-mates felt that pride for me – everybody did, except the management.'[5] Mandela (who in 1997 became the Honorary Patron of Malcolm's benefit year along with Michael Manley, the Prime Minister of Jamaica, thus framing a unique African-Caribbean and diasporan double) wrote a warm preface to Malcolm's benefit brochure, praising his career as an international cricketer and saying that he 'did England and South Africa proud on that tour.'[6] For Mandela, 'it was his integrity as a man that appealed to me most', and Malcolm's influence on young black South Africans was 'enormous' according to Ali Bacher, the Managing Director of the United Cricket Board of South Africa. After a spontaneous coaching session following the opening of the new clubhouse in Alexandria ex-township, Bacher explained how Malcolm had told the young cricketers that 'cricket taught confidence and self-esteem and that for the committed and gifted player cricket was a gateway to the world'.[7] That had certainly been the black Sheffielder's own real and true experience.

But it meant nothing to those who managed the South African tour. First, Malcolm was arbitrarily removed from the Soweto match and taken to Pretoria for special 'coaching sessions' from the bowling coach Peter Lever, who, in remarks to the travelling sporting press, labelled him a 'cricketing nonentity' whose bowling action needed to be re-moulded. Malcolm was bemused and shattered, so soon after his elation at meeting Mandela. He told me in October 1996 when I interviewed him for the *Observer*: 'When they took me out of the game in Soweto I felt that the congratulations from the President became to be used as the trigger for all that malice and bitterness. My team mates knew that the attention I was getting was for them too, the whole team. Only the management didn't understand that. So from my confidence being sky-high, I came crashing down when I heard what had been said to the journalists. I still suffer inside from that episode. I still get disturbing flashbacks of the insults and pain of it.' Another black man, vilified by the white managers and administrators appointed to lead and inspire him. No wonder his own white team mates defended and supported him. 'His treatment by the England management became intolerable', wrote Jack Russell later in Malcolm's benefit brochure. What they did was 'totally unjustified and unfair in the extreme', said Robin Smith, Devon's room-mate on the tour, a white man born in South Africa, now playing cricket for England. Later, after the last test, tour manager Ray Illingworth directly blamed England's defeat on Malcolm's bowling in an unprecedented and vitriolic personal attack. On his return from the tour and at the start of the 1996 season in England it was no wonder that he felt, both in cricketing and personal terms, 'on the floor'.

Yet despite these blows, 1996 proved to be one of Malcolm's most successful seasons with Derbyshire, his county side. Sloughing aside the bitterness of the England management, he took more wickets in the county game than any other bowler, excepting Gloucestershire's Jamaican fast bowler, Courtney Walsh. 'I found old and new sources of strength everywhere,' he explained. 'From my wife Jenny and our children, from my friends in the Sheffield community whom I knew were with me, and from my Derbyshire team-mates. I put all that treatment and insult out of my head. And I turned myself around.'

Perhaps his experiences high and low in South Africa have urged more reflection on the gentle destroyer. He remembers his own youth, after he came to Sheffield from Jamaica. He was never a 'natural', early-born cricketer: he made himself into a fast bowler, using his six feet two and a half inches and fifteen stone as his bulwarks of pace and fire. 'I didn't get to cricket until quite late,' he explains. 'I used to watch other people playing and think, 'I could do that, I could bowl quicker than that if I had the chance.' But it took me a long time.' He doesn't want the new generation of urban cricketers to work so long. 'Cricket is a great sport,' he posits: 'It can build anything and everything: patience, self-discipline, character. It's like life. These county and test matches are now for four and five days. That's a long time, like life is. So if you play it, just like in life you've got to have a strategy for it. How are you going to play it? How are you going to live it?' This cricket-spun philosophy reminded him of the days when he first played club cricket for the local Caribbean side in Sheffield. 'I used to think, 'I must do well, it's got to last me through the week!' And that's what used to happen. Each game built me up for the week which came after.'

Malcolm's sponsorship of the Sheffield inner city Devon Malcolm Cricket Centre gives him another living mission and enthusiasm. A part of his libel damages award from the Wisden Cricket Monthly case helps to keep it going, paying for essential equipment. 'It means so much to me that people wouldn't realise', he affirms. 'I want to put something back to young inner city people in cricket from the streets and estates that bred me.' I remember too, as headteacher of the local secondary school, the fascinated faces of a large group of young cricket devotees, girls and boys, as Malcolm used video to take them through – wicket by wicket – his 9-57 Oval triumph, reaching a power and articulacy in his words which matched his bowling feat.

It appeals to Malcolm that most of the young cricketers coming to the Centre are Pakistanis from the Fir Vale neighbourhood that surrounds the school, and that they are being coached by his old Sheffield United opening partner from the local Caribbean community, Steve Taylor. And Steve is quick too, as many bruised local batsman will attest. 'I played for Asian teams in Sheffield when I was up and coming,' remembers Malcolm. 'The Centre is for Pakistanis, Bangladeshis, West Indies, whites, Somalis, Yemenis – for anybody who wants to know the skills. Cricket teaches you respect for others. After I played with the Asian team, I got to know the players and their lives, their religion, their culture. That was all good and all happening because of cricket, binding people together in the community. I know too that the Centre and its work are preventing many young people from being sucked into the local drugs threat. If cricket can stop that and give an alternative that can build young people's lives then it's worth more than a sport.'

'Worth more than a sport,' worth a whole community. And 'community' is an important word for Malcolm. It has stayed at the centre of his cricket, all through his glory years. His old team-mates, the pioneers of the Sheffield Caribbean Club, are still very close to him and follow his achievements closely and lovingly. 'I can never forget them,' Devon admits, 'and I never will. I can't forget where all the hard work to make me into a cricketer was put in. They made sure I was a real cricketer. They helped me with everything. Not only my bowling and giving me the encouragement and skills, but they made sure I had transport for matches, they lent me equipment, they even gave me my tea money. How can I forget all that?'

'You must remember where you come from in cricket as in everything, and you must give back. These are the *true* people behind you, they follow and support you, they're *always* with you, urging you on, making you do better. It's the trust between you and them that's so important, because in the end you come back and you are one of them too. They are the people that give you most and who matter most.' I could hear again in Devon's message, C.L.R. James' essential dictum. 'The true cricketer will always come back to his community.'[8]

There are few people in professional cricket who have inspired so much warmth and admiration as Devon Malcolm. His gentleness, friendliness, self-discipline and loyal commitment to all those who play cricket and beyond, high and low, is almost legendary – despite the callous and arbitrary treatment he has received from England's cricket selectors and manager. His great South African fast bowling rival, the last of the 9-57, Allan Donald, declares, 'I would not make any bones about it when I say that I wish Devon played for South Africa. The man is a winner. He is an unlucky speed merchant who never got upset for being left out of an England team. For me, Devon is a friend whom I never got the chance to get close to.'[9]

But Devon has steel in him too, as Donald's fellow South Africans discovered at the Oval. He came to cricket from Sheffield, a great steel city, in Wincobank, a neighbourhood where most families had some working link with the steel industry. Now Wincobank is a rounded hill sticking out of north-east Sheffield where in times past, Celtic Brigante warriors withstood a long and brutal siege from the invading legions of the Roman empire. They held out in their fort at the summit of Wincobank hill, the same hill that bred in this same era the Yemeni-rooted world champion boxer 'Prince' Naseem Hamed, and the blistering pace of Devon Malcolm. Earth and steel, they make sports and those who revel in them.

Such a cricket reveller is Devon Malcolm, loved and respected by those who love his game precisely because when he plays it he is so generously human in what he does well and in what he does not so well. Vulnerable and unpredictable in his game, he has made both of these qualities into virtues. That is why we watch and hope with an added spark and grasp the sense of aspiration when he wilfully takes hold of the ball to bowl, or when he strides so fallibly to the wicket with a bat. He becomes the measure of all our own promises and fears, and we enter into every vein of his human struggle.

## REFERENCES

[1] See Devon Malcolm's autobiography, *You Guys Are History* (Collins Willow, London 1998) for detailed account of this incident.

[2] See *Devon Malcolm's Official Souvenir Beneift Brochure* (Holly Media Services, Derby, 1997)

[3] *Souvenir Beneift Brochure* as above.

[4] *Souvenir Beneift Brochure* as above.

[5] The interview extracts with Devon Malcolm were published (in part) in the *Observer*, 20 October 1996.

[6] Nelson Mandela's preface to *Souvenir Benefit Brochure*, as above.

[7] *Souvenir Beneift Brochure* as above.

[8] C.L.R. James, *Beyond a Boudary* (Serpent's Tail, London, 2000)

[9] *Souvenir Beneift Brochure* as above.

# 7.

# AMIR RIAZ
## Batting Against Barriers
## (1996)

THE SAME WEEKEND THAT RACISTS were despoiling the Second Test match at Headingley, Amir Riaz, a sixteen-year-old batsman from the Devon Malcolm Cricket Centre in inner city Sheffield, was showing the new spirit and creative talent of urban Yorkshire cricket. He was judged to be the top batsman of the tournament held at rural Arundel by the Lords' Taverners, which included teams from all over England. The legendary Gunn and Moore batmaking company of Nottingham, whose bats were used by all the old masters, will sponsor him for two years.

In the lordly presence of the veterans of the old game of cricket, 'the meadow game with the beautiful name' – Ted Dexter, Colin Cowdrey, Godfrey Evans – Amir demonstrated the energy and conviction of a reinvented game of the streets and urban waste ground, the tarmacked playgrounds, car parks and back alleys. Like dozens of his schoolmates in Fir Vale, north-eastern Sheffield, he has developed his batting and bowling skills partly through a huge cricketing motivation that runs through Yorkshire's Pakistani communities, and partly through the excellent mentoring of Steve Taylor, the Jamaican-born coach of the Devon Malcolm Centre – and Devon's old pace twin when they opened the bowling together for the local Caribbean side in the early eighties.

Fir Vale belies its name: there is little enough green to be seen. It is the echoing street that is Amir's venue. Bat and ball sound everywhere in the neighbourhood. Yet the Devon Malcolm Centre is taking raw, untutored talent and turning it into cricketing achievement. There are indoor nets in the local school's sports centre, smart equipment paid for by the donated winnings of Devon's case against the infamous article in *Wisden Cricket Monthly* (the Malcolm connection is not simply nominal), and regular matches at the well-groomed ground of the Caribbean club at the northern fringe of the city.

There is a particular quality to the cricket of Amir and his friends that the English game badly needs – and which would help to project it forward and throw off its present incubus. It arises out of inner city cricket itself: a certain boundless creative energy and confidence, coming from young people who are unafraid to challenge old barriers, are prepared to be innovative and who refuse to bow to timeworn shibboleths. It is a cricket which overcomes.

Amir and his friends know the unwelcome boundaries marked out against their entry into the representative game in Yorkshire. They have few illusions and can defend and play for themselves. Yet as young black and urban cricketers they are eager to break through. And they play that way, like Amir and his pure and exuberant drives, his zest and power of bat and brain, the determined trajectory of his seam bowling.

His parents came to Yorkshire from a village near Islamabad, but Amir was made in Sheffield. His father was a steelworker for many years, before running a taxi firm. When Amir went to Pakistan for a holiday he was amazed to see cricket played absolutely everywhere – even more than in Fir Vale. 'Whenever the lads find any little spaces, they're out there playing,' he said. 'Seeing that made me even more keen to improve'.

In Fir Vale though, there are other, more menacing distractions. Amir has been inspired by Steve Taylor to want to become a coach himself. 'Steve has taught me everything,' he says. 'So now I want to coach the younger lads. Drugs are a serious problem in this part of the city. I have seen how cricket has taken many boys away from them. I want to make sure that it carries on doing that. It's taught them a better way to approach their life'.

His two favourite batsmen are Javed Miandad and Alec Stewart. He admires the attacking mode of Stewart but models himself on Miandad: 'I liked the way he used to adapt himself to any conditions. He could be aggressive and determined, but also humorous on the pitch. It was his confident style I liked – that's what I'd like for my own batting'.

He loves the unfettered feeling of driving the ball: the cover drive is his number one stroke, he says. At Arundel he was presented with his first Gunn and Moore bat by Godfrey Evans: 'I tried it out yesterday with my friends. I just took it and started driving with it – the middle was right perfect, just beautiful. It felt so strong and you should have seen the ball go!'

There is something just and fitting that the bat of the patriarchs of cricket should now be in the powerful and intelligent hands of young inner city cricketers like Amir. It is as if grasping the past, they now hold the future of English cricket and its revival before them. Amir aspires to play for Yorkshire like so many of his friends. Yorkshire is lucky to have them, and so is England – although the road to realisation seems a long and painful one.

As for Amir, he knows that he will have 'to try twice as hard and play twice as well' to make it. But he now has a bat of history in his grip to help him make a new cricketing future.

# 8.

## MURALI'S MATCH
### The Oval, August 1998
### (1999)

HE BOWLED WITH ONE OF THE STRANGEST actions in living and written memory. His bowling arm bent through a hereditary deformity, his double-jointed wrist putting his delivery hand at right angles to his forearm, a quivering flick of his braceleted wrist as he let go of the ball, a flight that looped and buzzed, the impact of the ball on the turf taking sudden and unconscionable directions at prodigious angles. Thus did Muttiah Muralitharan, a confectioner's son from Kandy, Sri Lanka, confound the England batsman at London's Oval Cricket Ground in August 1998. His match figures of 16 wickets for 220 runs, including 9 for 65 in England's second innings, provoked a landslide of the home nation's batting and a famous victory in only Sri Lanka's second test match on English soil. It set the poetic impulses of the cricket writers ticking out loud. David Hopps of the *Guardian* wrote of Muralitharan's 'wrist like a revolving door'[1], while Peter Roebuck of *The Cricketer* declared that 'he made the ball fall like a shot bird'[2].

Although a caption under a *Guardian* photo of the 'destroyer' bowler who 'beat England virtually single-handed and double jointed'[3] was something of an exaggeration, his contribution was unique and immense. It was, as the paper reported, sporting achievement of 'sheer genius', shared by his team-mates. There was the patient, classic century by batsman Aravinda de Silva paired with the explosive double century by opener Sanath Jayasuriya, full of original stroke play and an inventive batting choreography, as Sri Lankan in its character as Rohan Kanhai's innovations had been so effusively Guyanese and Caribbean in the sixties. The two sixes that he hit in his brief second innings of 24 to take his country's score past that of England were shots that were invented in the moments that they were executed. No one watching had seen their like before: an audacious flick to leg off Fraser that soared over the ropes towards Vauxhall Station and a square cut off Hollioake carved out momentarily in mid-air as Jayasuriya took flight on the spot and propelled his bat to meet the ball with a beautiful but untrammeled force. It was cricket in creative process, an innings as a workshop. Here were cricketing moments to last a lifetime, as were the lightning reflexes and speared throw of Upul Chandana that ran out Alec Stewart in England's second innings.

It was a victory of outstanding all-round excellence from an international team the *Guardian* leader writer described as 'the most thrilling' in world cricket. Yet how had they been treated by their old imperial rulers and the game of cricket they still controlled? In 1996 they had become world champions of the one-day game, yet, as the leader continued, in 1998 'they were only allowed to play in a one-day tournament if the South Africans took part as well, as a sort of chaperon, and they were granted just the one measly test yet again'[4]. And as their performance and result revealed, the only measly element was some of their English hosts' response to their brilliance. 'There is also the vague smell of (probably sub-conscious) racism', the *Guardian* observed: 'Much safer to ask the (still mainly white) South Africans to play a full series than the little brown men with the unpronounceable names. They are still not pronounced right. For the first time in memory, neither the BBC radio nor television had a commentator from the visiting country. It was a symbol of our attitude towards Sri Lanka. Defeat serves us right.'

The writer was referring to the one test match offered to Sri Lanka, tacked on to the full series of five tests, given to the post-Apartheid but still predominantly white South African team. But in the aftermath of Sri Lanka's victory other draughts of racism were felt across English cricket. David 'Bumble' Lloyd, England's coach, was quoted in the *Daily Mail* as declaring: 'I have my opinion and will make it known to the authorities. That is as far as I will go. We have a leg-spinner with an orthodox action. They have an off-spinner with an unorthodox action'[5]. This was roundly interpreted across the cricket world as an innuendo attacking the legitimacy of Muralitharan's bowling action, suggesting that he was 'throwing' the ball against the laws of the game, rather than 'bowling' it. Although these 'splutterings', as 'Bouncer' in *The Cricketer*[6] called them, were seen as the response of a defeated and piqued eccentric, and Lloyd was reprimanded by the England Cricket Board,[7] they were both hurtful and offensive to the Sri Lankans. Muralitharan's action had been exhaustively examined by the International Cricket Council, the sport's governing body. He was repeatedly photographed from six different angles at 1000 frames a second by a study group from the University of Western Australia and was fully cleared. His examiners declared that any resemblance to throwing was an 'optical illusion'[8] caused by the deformity from birth in both his arms which prevented his elbow being fully straightened. The accusation of being a 'chucker' had temporarily dented his confidence, but not prevented him from reaching over 200 wickets from a mere 42 test matches, a remarkable record.

Lloyd's underhand suggestions were strongly refuted by the majority of cricket writers, with the exception of Peter Hayter of the *Mail On Sunday*,[9] and dramatically contradicted by the fulsome praise for Muralitharan from the England captain Alec Stewart, who saluted the bowler's achievement. 'They out-played us, and one bloke bowled magnificently', he told *The Times*[10]. 'He spun the ball more than any spinner I have ever known. He is a special bowler, in a league of his own'[11]. Yet even in the overwhelming accolades given to Muralitharan, Jayasuriya and De Silva, a close reading of their texts revealed a discomforting tone, and the old, pervasive undercurrents of imperial racism were still flowing, however deep beneath the surface. Despite his acknowledgement of Sri Lanka's 'charming team' and Muralitharan, *The Times* cricket correspondent Michael Henderson, writing in *The Cricketer*, applauded the 'true craft' of brilliant off-spinners. 'No matter where they come from, they should be applauded,' he declared. '*No matter where they come from*'[12] – even Sri Lanka? The implications were obvious, subliminal and profoundly insulting.

Even the official Souvenir Programme of the Oval Test Match introduced Muralitharan as a 'cricketing freak' – recalling the description given of black New Zealand rugby match-winner Jonah Lomu by 1995 England World Cup captain Will Carling. Lomu, declared Carling, was also a 'freak' who had won the World Cup for New Zealand. And amongst the writing about Muralitharan were strange, irrational statements coming from the 'voice of cricket' and world's best-selling cricket journal, founded in 1921, almost as if there were something devilish or superstitious about him, some dark, primitive power from 'out there' that he was fixing on English batsmen. Here was Peter Roebuck writing in *The Cricketer*, under the title of *Sri Lankan Sorcerer*:

> *At any moment one expected a black cat to fly by or a witch to start stirring a brew. This was not the sorcerer's apprentice; it was the sorcerer himself, weaving spells, uttering his odes .... At times he might have been working to the beat of jungle drums.*
>
> *And all the while the sorcerer wheeled away, his mischievous grin lightening his face, flinging the ball into the air, hiding it in his hands as he ran into bowl, gripping it with his middle fingers and all the while creating the impression of malevolence.*[13]

An extraordinary piece of cricket writing, this. Imbuing the bowler – as Roebuck later elaborates – with the power of 'mystique' and atavistic 'darkness' which the writer compares to a similar potency held in common with the former Pakistani spinner Abdul Qadir and an unnamed 'youngster' who is 'emerging in India'. No comparisons are drawn with outstanding white spinners like Laker of England, Warne or Grimmett of Australia, or Tayfield of South Africa. It is as if this primal and uncanny power is something of the Orient, evincing a 'capacity which is beyond our comprehension' as English cricketers – combined of course with Muralitharan's 'freakish collection of physical abilities'. Similar attributes were projected to the 'East Indian' Trinidadian spinner K.T. 'Sonny' Ramadhin after he had whittled through the England batting several times during the West Indies tour of England in 1950. There were similar efforts made by cricket writers to prefer to describe his prodigious talent in terms of 'magic'[14] or the irrational rather than sheer talent, innovation and artistry. Even a writer such as Clayton Goodwin, who studied within the School of Oriental and African Studies at the University of London, wrote in his book, *Caribbean Cricketers*, that 'everything about him (Ramadhin) was a mystery'[15]. It took a writer from Ramadhin's own Indo-Caribbean community to recognise what real powers lay behind Ramadhin's apparent 'mystery'. As well as his remarkable ability to spin the ball and disguise his spin, wrote Frank Birbalsingh in his *Indo-West Indian Cricket*, Ramadhin 'on perfectly good wickets could dismiss batsmen through a combination of accurate length, unerring direction and crafty variations of flight'[16]. It was a rational analysis of the craft of spin bowling that could also be applied to Muralitharan in 1998.

Yet beyond the mystification that was emitted around him by English cricket writers, Muralitharan was a lone Sri Lankan Tamil in a team comprised of Sinhalese. His achievement, and the acknowledgement and admiration of it by his team mates and particularly by his captain, the veteran Arjuna Ranatunga who had led Sri Lanka for a decade, was in itself a symbolic blow against Sri Lankan communalism.

Writing in his *Souls of Black Folk* in 1903, the great grandson of an American slave, activist and intellectual W.E.B. Du Bois, identified 'the world-old phenomenon of the contact of diverse races'[17] and the consequences of 'war, murder, slavery, extermination and debauchery' which had characterised racist power relations, as the major social and political dimension of the new century. At the outset of this new century, it is clear that the struggle against racism and the pursuit of racial justice by those directly afflicted by it and their allies, will continue to be a dominant theme of life and progress. But it will be accompanied by a parallel struggle that will mark the new century and the new millennium – a contest, in many large and small places of the world, to break the deadly hold of communalism. In Palestine, in Ireland, in the Balkans, in Indonesia, in India, Rwanda, Somalia and other African nations, in the great cities, urban conurbations and wastelands of North America and Europe – communal conflicts have raged in the mid and dying years of the twentieth century – and with no greater ferocity than in the island of Sri Lanka.

This communalist violence has been described and anatomized most acutely and with living knowledge as well as heart-felt insight in the writings of the Sri Lankan political analyst and novelist, A. Sivanandan – like Muralitharan, from the Tamil minority. In his essay *Sri Lanka: A Case Study*, Sivanandan wrote of the communalism in his country in this way, taking particular care to discriminate between communal violence and the violence of the state:

*Communalism implies a parallel relationship between communal groups, antagonistic perhaps but not necessarily unequal.... Communal violence, therefore, refers to that which occurs between (communal) groups, not to that inflicted on one group by the state, representing another. Hence, the use of the term (communal) 'riots', when what is meant – or should be – is state pogroms. This is not just a euphemism but a violent distortion of the truth – which further adds to the pretended innocence of the state. Communalism is an 'afraid' word.*

*Communalism is also a portmanteau word. It takes in all the dirty linen of religion, language, culture, 'ethnicity'. And it is a flat word, one-dimensional – gives no idea of the dynamics of relationships within a country or between communities.[18]*

To experience the process of that same 'flatness' achieving visceral meaning and affective power in the written word through the crucible of the Sri Lankan historical imagination, the reader must turn to Sivanandan's novel *When Memory Dies*[19]. In its pages the shards of people's lives, broken to pieces by the colonial imposition and directed towards communalist hatred, racism against Tamils as 'infidels of a degraded race'[20] and unremitting state violence, are given epic expression. For the world evoked in this novel of imperial oppression, colonial division, the roots of ethnic preference and the power that ordinary people of all communities have within them to struggle and unite through trade unions, anti-colonial resistance and their own human love – all mighty anti-deterministic forces and mechanisms – is most movingly and instructively set down.

Out of that history and continuity of Sinhala/Tamil communal conflict and the common struggle of its antidote, Sri Lanka has been born, with all its institutions and cultural manifestations, including its cricket. Muttiah Muralitharan is a Sri Lankan Tamil playing cricket for his country – a national sport dominated and controlled largely by Sinhala power. This has made the scope of his achievement all the greater, and his example all the more extraordinary and compelling. His Sinhala team mates, led by Ranatunga, continue to marvel at his contribution to Sri Lankan cricket and have been quick to point out how little he has been appreciated by the industrial and commercial interests which underwrite the professional game. Comparing the support from his own country's cricket sponsors to that coming to the Australian spinner, Shane Warne, from his own national commercial supporters, Ranatunga exposed to what level Muralitharan is being virtually ignored. 'A local businessman sponsors his bat for a few pounds', said Ranatunga, and this is all. 'It's very sad'[21], he added.

In January 1999 the Sri Lanka captain showed his powerful solidarity with his Tamil team-mate when Muralitharan was no-balled for 'throwing' by the Australian umpire Darrell Hair at the Adelaide test match. He rallied the entire team and led them to the edge of the field of play in protest at the umpire's decision, which had been taken in the face of the International Cricket Council's clearance of the bowler's action. Ranatunga declared to the world's sporting press: 'I felt I was doing the right thing by a colleague of mine who has been the best bowler Sri Lanka has ever produced'[22]. With these words Ranatunga publicly challenged and defied communalism and separation in his nation's sporting culture, as Muralitharan himself had done symbolically over 200 times – in every test match wicket he had taken in the company of his Sinhala team-mates over the previous four years.

In his own way, and in his own particular theatre of public life, Ranatunga had struck a blow against what Sivanandan had described as the 'degeneracy of Sinhala society and its rapid descent into barbarism'[23] against Tamil neighbours and fellow citizens. That this small but emblematic advance in human unity and social progress against communalism took place on a cricket field with all its drama, emotion and artistry, makes a strong statement about the symbolic excellence of sport – and in particular, cricket itself, the imperial game, transformed and reinvented by those whom its original masters intended to subject.

## REFERENCES

[1] *Guardian* (1 September 1998)

[2] *The Cricketer* (October 1998)

[3] *Guardian* (1 September 1998)

[4] Ibid.

[5] *Daily Mail* (1 September 1998)

[6] *The Cricketer* (October 1998)

[7] *Evening Standard* (1 September 1998)

[8] See the feature on Muralitharan in the official *Souvenir Programme of the Oval Test Match* (England Cricket Board, London 1998)

[9] *Mail On Sunday* (6 September 1998)

[10] *The Times* (1 September 1998)

[11] *Guardian* (1 September 1998)

[12] *The Cricketer* (October 1998)

[13] *The Cricketer* (October1998)

[14] See David Sheppard, *Parson's Pitch* (London 1964)

[15] Clayton Goodwin, *Carribean Cricketers from the Pioneers to Packer* (London 1980)

[16] Frank Birbalsingh and Clem Shiwcharan, *Indo-West Indian Cricket* (London 1998)

[17] W.E.B. Du Bois, *Souls of Black Folk* (1903)

[18] A. Sivanandan, 'Sri Lanka: A Case Study' from *Communities of Resistance* (London, 1990)

[19] Ibid.

[20] Ibid.

[21] *Guardian* (1 September 1998)

[22] *Guardian* (26 January 1999)

[23] A. Sivanandan, `Sri Lanka: A Case Study' from *Communities of Resistance* (London, 1990)

# 9.

# AUSTRALIA LAKERED...
# ENGLAND NASSERED!
## Cricket and the Suez crisis of 1956
## (2000)

WATCHING THEM ON OUR SMALL BLACK and white television screen in the summer of 1956, they seemed a forlorn and despairing procession, these men of the greatest of the Empire's sporting nations. As *The Times* reported on its cricket pages the next day: 'The Australians came out one by one to the slaughter convinced, it seemed, before they took strike, that they had not long to live'.[1] Re-working the old racist rhyme, the *Daily Express* ran its triumphant headline: 'Ten little Aussie boys Lakered in a Row'[2], and the dry-humoured off-spinning Yorkshireman, Jim Laker, had taken nineteen Australian wickets in the Fourth Test Match at Old Trafford, Manchester, out of a possible twenty, and achieved the most staggering bowling success ever in a single international cricket match.

This was during the last week of July. To the English press and those who played and loved the imperial game, the victory over the sporting enemy represented the zenith of the mother nation's cricket fortunes, just as the defeat of 1882 at Lords and the burning of the 'Ashes' had been its nadir. It was, as the *Picture Post* described in their celebratory pamphlet, 'the most amazing day in the history of test cricket'[3]. Laker, bowling his prodigious off breaks with relentless accuracy and turning them at the sharpest of angles had given England 'the stuff of which fantasies are made', and offered a crutch to a nation that was beginning to spill its colonized territories all over the world. Never mind the communist 'terrorists' in Malaya, the Mau-Mau conspirators in Kenya or the EOKA guerrillas in the Cypriot mountains, national confidence had been restored by sporting success. For as one of his test match victims twice over in the match, the future Australia captain and renowned cricket commentator Richie Benaud, declared, Laker's victory went far beyond cricket, as 'he was cheered all over England, not only by cricket supporters but by the man in the street'[4]. The panoply of imperial equilibrium was thus temporarily re-constructed and England were victorious again on the pitch of the world.

Led by the outstanding batsman of his generation, Peter May, of the public school Charterhouse and Pembroke College, Cambridge, who during the test series amassed 453 runs at an average of over ninety, the England side which won at Old Trafford was one of the strongest in the history of cricket. The first five of the batting order were holding on to the status of 'amateurs'. Two of them – Peter Richardson of Worcestershire and the Reverend David Sheppard – who had been recalled to the Test match side after his ordination into the Anglican priesthood and only a handful of first class games behind him during the summer – scored centuries; while the bowling attack of Laker and his Surrey 'spin twin' Tony Lock and the indefatigable fast bowler Brian Statham (all professionals) represented the cream of English bowling. Other outstanding bowlers like Fred Trueman, and the Northamptonshire velocipede, Frank Tyson, could not even make selection while great batsmen of a previous era, Denis Compton and Cyril Washbrook, made impressive comebacks during the test matches. England had an embarrassment of cricketing talent and were now truly world leaders in the game which they had invented and for which they were renowned in every crumbling corner of the Empire.

Yet on the day Laker's test match began, July 26, other events were sparking mass applause too in other parts of the world. The date was the anniversary of the 1952 Revolution in Egypt, when the 'Free Officers' movement had deposed the corrupt international socialite King Farouk and established a new dispensation, dedicated to land reform and ridding the country of foreign, exploitative interest – much of which was English. The titular leader of this movement was the apparently avuncular fifty-year-old General Muhammed Neguib, but its real leader was the nationalist and Pan Arabist Gamal Abdul Nasser, the son of a poor peasant of upper Egypt.

Nasser's father had eventually gained a primary school certificate and become a post office official. His son's *fellah* background made him an inspirational figure in a military command structure still dominated by the arrogant sons of *pashas, beys* and other ruling class offspring.

On Thursday, July 26, during the Fourth Anniversary celebrations, Nasser made a two and a half-hour speech in Menshira'h Square, Alexandria. As Richardson and Colin Cowdrey put on 174 for England's first wicket and Jim Laker sat on the players' balcony at Old Trafford waiting for his moment, Egypt's leader announced his government's nationalisation of the Suez Canal, certainly the world's most strategic waterway and historically Britain's passage to its empire. His declaration provoked a ten-minute ovation and united the Egyptian people and their parties, right and left, behind him. More than 80% of the canal's shareholders were either British or French. As Nasser finished his speech and sought to leave the square, he was mobbed by supporters. A US consul who was present described the aftermath of the furore of adulation – a large celebratory float stood in the square of a `Sphinx swallowing a British soldier with the British flag sewn on his derriere'[5].

As a twelve-year-old boy at the time who had little understanding of these events and their causes, I was astonished at the sudden surge of indignation and hatred that overtook the English people and which in an instant found expression in all the newspapers. Nasser became the prototype of the hated Arab that has been thematic in the second half of the nineteenth century and found similar levels of vitriol in the media and public portraiture of Gaddaffi, Arafat and finally, Saddam. The fact that the Suez Canal ran directly through Egyptian national territory became irrelevant to outraged English public opinion.

The Prime Minister, Anthony Eden, was an Oxford man with an aristocratic lineage. He was also an orientalist, having read Arabic Studies for his degree, and spoke the language fluently. When news of Nasser's nationalisation speech arrived in London after close of play at Old Trafford, Eden was holding a Downing Street dinner party for 'friendly' Arab leaders of the Baghdad Pact, King Feisal of Iraq and his Anglophile Prime Minister Nuri es-Said, who had been a close friend of the Prime Minister for three decades. The Prime Minister led the national apoplexy that was directed towards the Egyptian leader, and provoked the old imperial racism which frequently characterised British attitudes towards the Arab peoples. I can remember family conversations expressing a horrific indignation at Nasser's 'bloody cheek', at the sheer impertinence of claiming what 'Europeans' had financed, engineered and built for the sake of 'international trade'. He was not to be allowed 'to have his hand on our windpipe', proclaimed Eden, 'Nasser must be broken.... This should be accomplished with economic and political means. If, however, these are tried and proved insufficient, the UK should then use armed force'. The Foreign Secretary, Selwyn Lloyd, soon joined in. Nasser was a 'paranoiac', he declared, 'and had the same type of mind as Hitler'. The Hitler comparison was also seized upon by the French military and government. Guy Mollet, the French Prime Minister, likened Nasser's purchase of arms from the Soviet Union to the 1939 Hitler-Stalin Pact and the canal nationalisation to the Fuhrer's seizure of the Rhineland. Eden wrote to Eisenhower, the US President, that 'I have no doubt that the Bear is using Nasser... he must not be allowed to get away with it'[6]. Indeed, the Prime Minister's frenzied and irrational response to Nasser's 'act of plunder' reached as far as an assassination plan drafted by M16, involving the injection of nerve gas into Nasser's office, and suggestions that the Egyptian's coffee should be poisoned.

Eden's hawkishness was strongly supported by warmongering statements from Chancellor of the Exchequer Harold Macmillan, who declared that 'if the Canal result was to be the destruction of Great Britain as (a) first class power... the danger should be met now... if we should be destroyed by Russian bombs now that would be better than to be reduced to impotence'. There was much talk among politicians and public of going it alone and 'going all the way' to crush Nasser, and Eden soon had all-party support, with Labour opposition leader Hugh Gaitskell matching his anger across the dispatch box. In the parliamentary debate of August 2, Gaitskell opined: 'this episode must be recognised as part of the struggle for the mastery of the Middle East... It is exactly the same that we encountered from Mussolini and Hitler in those years before the war'[7].

Thus confusion and intense contradiction scored the news stories of the front and back pages of British newspapers during that final week in July and the first week of August. Sporting glory and political humiliation: the Australians Lakered, the British Nassered. Yet Australian help for the furious British government was soon at hand in the person of the affable Sir

Robert Menzies, the pro-British, conservative and cricket-loving Australian Prime Minister. On August 16 a conference involving delegates of twenty national governments was held in London to attempt to find a solution to the crisis in Egypt. The US, through Secretary of State John Foster Dulles, took the lead in putting forward proposals which would retain international control of the canal, give compensation for the Canal Company and maintain the guarantee of freedom of navigation for ships of all nations. Dulles also made it clear to the world's press that the US government had no wish to go to war over Nasser's nationalisation, and was determined to achieve a peaceful settlement – a part of Eisenhower's strategy to impress the rising numbers of independent and decolonised nations of the US' 'peacekeeping' international ambitions: 'We must make a genuine effort to bring world opinion to favour the international control of the Canal', he declared. In this way Nasser would be compelled to 'disgorge what he had attempted to swallow'. Thus Menzies, with his staunch and vaunted loyalty to Britain and its own Conservative government, travelled to Cairo to meet Nasser with a toothless hope, knowing that the US had already detached itself from taking part in any military solution. So this time on Egyptian soil, Australia faced further loss and humiliation – while at the Oval in London, it was only bad light which saved the Australian cricket team from defeat again in the final test match of the summer, with Laker again biting deep into the Australian batting and finishing the series with 46 wickets, more than any other bowler had ever achieved in a single test match series against Australia. England had defeated Australia for the prize of the 'Ashes' for the third time in succession, and felt on top of the cricketing world. The Australian cricketers returned to their homeland to contemplate their own government's generosity to that of Britain in allowing them to test atomic bombs and lay nuclear waste to vast areas of their country, and to consider the racist implications of a 'White Australia Policy' and their treatment of native Australians. 'In 1956, if somebody coloured walked down Market Place in Sydney,' revealed ex-Immigration Minister Arthur Calwell to Australian journalist John Pilger, 'he would be at the centre of all attention. So I rejected him for two reasons... one for Australia's sake and the other for himself, so he wouldn't be embarrassed and treated badly'[8].

Meanwhile, Britain's public opinion was suppurating with its own racist appetite towards Nasser and Egypt, stoked up by an arm of the Foreign

Office - 'The Information Research Department', which was working in close liaison with military intelligence services and providing the BBC with negative and scurrilous material about Nasser. This was transmitted through radio frequencies from Aden, Cyprus and Libya, and a 'friendly' Iraqi announcer was calling for Nasser's assassination. The opening bars of Beethoven's Fifth Symphony (recalling broadcasts made by the anti-Hitler allies during the Second World War) now became the signature tune for the anti-Nasser broadcasts as the radio destabilization campaign was networked through pro-British airwaves throughout the Arab world. The anti-Arabism and Islamophobia so familiar to British newspaper readers of the 1990s was laying down foundations in the press campaigns against the Egyptian leader during the late summer of 1956. The vicious cartoons in *Punch*[9] led the way, with Nasser caricatured as a devilish-looking Imam preaching from the minaret of a mosque, that 'Nasser is great and Suez is his profit'. As preparations were already being made for the eventual military expedition 'Musketeer' to regain the Canal Zone, the same journal printed what it called a 'Troop Deck Ballad' in August 1956. This purported to express the attitudes of the British army reservists en route for the invasion of Egypt 'to bolster up the shares in the Canal' and take it back for Britain. In well-versed doggerel redolent of the era of Kipling and Rhodes, but carrying through the continuity of imperial racism, its lyrics promised to 'knock this dastard Nasser to the middle of next week', and continued in its final verse:

> *There's another whole division coming*
> *out to fight the wogs*
> *(And a squadron's-worth of Canberras no*
> *further off than Malta)*
> *And three small aircraft carriers to*
> *Show the dirty dogs*
> *Who owns the Med from Jaffa to Gibraltar.*
> *For the serried ranks of Gyppos (backed*
> *By Jordan and Iraq)*
> *Are Egyptians we'll be very glad to spoil,*
> *When the voice that breathes from Eden*
> *Says we've got to have a crack*

> *So the motorists of England shall never*
> *Lack for oil.*[10]

.

Intoxicated on a cocktail of rampant jingoism, sporting success and racist belligerence, British public sympathies for an expedition against Nasser's 'sauce' were buoyed up and ready for action.

Yet world political opinion was a different matter. Nasser was being saluted as a hero by the leaders of many non-aligned and shortly-to-be decolonised nations. The US had already made clear its preference for a negotiated option with the involvement of the United Nations. Britain's Atlantic ally and 'best friend' saw its own imperial objectives in less directly military terms, and was not for proceeding in the old 'British' way, already foreseeing that any coming conflict could leave the 'neutral' US the true inheritor of Britain's old imperial role. The canny Dulles saw different divisive strategies commanded by the economic strength and leadership of the US which, while learning much from the old 'divide and rule' British imperial hallmark, would work in different, less immediately militaristic and gunboat ways. 'There are economic pressures, which, if continued, will cause distress in Egypt', he instructed Eden in a diplomatic note, 'There are Arab rivalries to be exploited and which can be exploited if we don't make Nasser an Arab hero'[11]. Ironically, Dulles' strategy had already been defeated by the equally sharp and wily Nasser. On July 19, when the US (and on the following day, Britain) had decided to pull out of large scale economic assistance for Egypt's projected Aswan Dam scheme which would make the nation self sufficient in electricity supply as well as increase its arable land by one sixth, Nasser had duly and successfully turned to the Soviets for economic support. The lowly-born Egyptian's tactical adroitness in playing off east and west had triggered Eden's spleen with even greater bursts of vituperation:

'I don't care a damn if there's anarchy and chaos in Egypt,' he spluttered to Anthony Nutting, a young Foreign Office Minister, over the telephone: 'I want him destroyed, can't you understand?'.[12]

So a pretext for the destruction of this turbulent Arab and the swift restitution of 'our' canal had to be found, or invented. The scam that was eventually devised was certainly 'not cricket', and probably one of the most dishonest, secretive and inglorious (as well as spectacularly unsuccessful) ruses that British imperialism (combined with its French counterpart) ever concocted, even in its fading days. The strategy involved employing Israel, the west's creation and buffer in the Arab world, to act as the main *agent provocateur*. Egypt's 1948 war against Israel's new polity had resulted in Egyptian defeat and a spur to the Free Officers to build their movement to overturn the feudal state led by Farouk's corrupt and demeaning monarchy. On August 22 conflict was rekindled with Israel, recently under a new government led by David Ben-Gurion, when Israeli forces crossed into Egypt and occupied parts of the Gaza Strip. Nasser, now undisputed as the leader of militant Pan-Arabism, and as such the aspirant protector of 900,000 Palestinian refugees, was viewed more and more as the dominant threat to Israeli statehood. Thus Britain and France had a mechanism to use to trigger conflict with an Egypt growing in regional and international prestige and leadership, led by a man who had challenged their traditional imperial roles. France, still smouldering from defeat by the Vietnamese at Dien Bien Phu in 1954, was seeking to militarily defuse an insurgent Algerian nationalism which was strongly supported by Nasser's government, and in 1955 had supplied seventy-two Mystere fighter aircraft, tanks and other arms to the Israeli military. Israel felt ready to challenge Nasser, and had a Chief of Staff, the hawk Moshe Dayan, who was inviting 'an early confrontation with the Egyptian regime, which is striving toward a war for the destruction of Israel'[13].

The plan was cobbled together between the French and English governments on October 14. Israel would be secretly urged by its allies to attack Egyptian territory on the Sinai Peninsula. Britain and France, acting jointly, would then order the belligerents, Israel and Egypt, to stop fighting and withdraw their armies to at least ten miles either side of the Canal Zone, which would then be temporarily occupied by Anglo-French forces, masquerading as peacekeepers. These plans were secretly elaborated and affirmed by representatives of the British, French and Israeli governments at Sevres, just outside Paris, on October 21. In an act of calculated deception of Parliament, public and even senior civil servants and military commanders, Eden's government had clandestinely colluded with France and Israel and decided upon a protocol which was an actual declaration of war against Nasser and Egypt, with the Anglo-French plans already laid for the invasion and occupation of Port Said and called 'Operation Omelette'.

Selwyn Lloyd later admitted in his *Suez 1956* that, 'If I thought it would save British lives, protect British property and serve British interests to conceal part of the facts from Parliament, I would not hesitate for a moment to do so'. Eden, however, goaded by opposition questioning in December 1956, was adamant in his concealment and economy with the truth: 'I want to say on this question of foreknowledge and say it quite bluntly to the House, that there was not foreknowledge that Israel would attack Egypt – there was not'[14]. The mother of parliaments was listening to the mother of lies from perhaps the last unambiguously imperial of British prime ministers, whose duplicity signalled another blast of the 'winds of change' that a prominent successor, Harold Macmillan, was to invoke years later at the opposite tip of that great continent where British troops had vainly invaded in the autumn of 1956. Ironically, when the *Observer* leader writer described the monumental deception as 'such folly and crookedness'[15] in its edition of November 4, it was using words usually employed to describe the genre of ambitious Third World regimes, one of which Britain itself was now seeking to destabilise and destroy.

In 1956 Britain had 750,000 men under arms and spent ten per cent of its gross national product on defence[16]. Yet after a mere 36 hours of military action around Port Said a halt was called to the invasion of November 5, with the Anglo-French forces a mere twenty-five miles south of their landing position. By November 23, Eden, the shattered and politically defeated Prime Minister of Britain and its Empire, was recuperating in Jamaica, staying at the home of his friend Ian Fleming, the author of the James Bond books and 007 fantasist whose creation was to become the chimera of a lost British global prestige and audacity. It seemed that it was only in cricket that England ruled the world, and only temporarily at that. Nasser, far from being defeated and isolated, the purpose of the powers that invaded his nation, at home and across the Arab and non-aligned world became an icon, his reputation hugely enhanced by the success of his anti-imperial 'impudence' – the absolute antithesis of the hopes of his enemies. The invading allies had been unable to withstand the buffeting of world opinion and the aggressive disapproval of their strongest ally, the eventual beneficiary of the debacle, both diplomatic and military, which they had perpetrated. Now Egypt had no barriers to the taking over of the 15,000 plus British and French enterprises in Egypt, and securing the final closure of the large British military base in the Canal Zone, for there was no greater symbol of the European imperial power in the Arab world than the Suez Canal. Now, through Anglo-French folly and his own astuteness, Nasser had won for Arabs a total diplomatic victory. As Albert Hourani observed in his *History of the Arab Peoples*[17], he 'appeared in the eyes of most Arabs and much of the outside world, as the symbol of the movement of Arab peoples towards greater unity and genuine independence"

Suez in 1956 was the last great watershed of British imperial influence, not only in the Middle East, but also throughout the rest of Africa, Asia and the Americas. As a final curtain of British dominance, it left the stage clear for the new imperial protagonist, the USA, to assert new forms of hegemony during the coming decades. In the massive coverage of the fiasco and its aftermath, the exploits of Laker, May and his team were soon little more than symbolic memories of a time just before a disastrous divorce with history, a swansong of glorious sporting nostalgia soon to be ruefully and totally eclipsed even on the cricket field, when Australia was to regain the Ashes during the 1958-9 English tour. Britain had finished its 1956 summer with its national self-confidence intact and strengthened by its sporting heroes, still retaining a belief in a mythical notion of God-given superiority over those who lived 'out there' and who for centuries had been seen as the 'subject races'. It is not an exaggeration to say that the personality and audacity of Gamal Abdul Nasser was a prime mover in shaking that sense of longstanding national assurance to its foundations.

In the English cricket universe, too, new questions were being raised which had a direct bearing on the aftermath of Suez. Racist assumptions centred upon Nasser had been exploded as a direct result of the crisis and, as May, Laker (who rare among cricketers of his generation was to strongly condemn apartheid) and the English touring team left for South Africa in the autumn of 1956, other huge issues were, at last, coming to the fore within the sport. These were surfacing around the personality of David Sheppard, the first ordained priest to score a century in a test match – in fact in Laker's test match at Old Trafford in July. The 'question which hurt' Sheppard most, as he later put it in his autobiography, *Parson's Pitch*[18], was whether to play cricket against a lily-white South African team, picked on the basis of white racial superiority and black exclusion as the direct expression of Apartheid law. Sheppard was not a militant antiracist, but an active and sincere Christian much influenced by Biblical text and its human manifestation. He later wrote that his final decision to make a public protest against Apartheid was provoked by a reading of Isaiah, 'Loose the bonds of wickedness, to undo the thongs of the yoke, to let the oppressed go free'. But that was to be in the future, in 1960, the year of the massacre of 69 black South Africans at Sharpeville in the Transvaal, which more than any other event opened up the racist terror and injustice of South Africa to the entire world.

In 1956 after his batting success at Old Trafford, Sheppard was an obvious candidate for selection for the tour of South Africa. He declared that he was not available due to his work as an Anglican priest in London's Islington. The cricket correspondent of the *News Chronicle*, Crawford White, suspected there were other motives of conscience stopping Sheppard's participation on the tour, and after interviewing him published an article headlined 'I won't play in Africa'. Sheppard's reticence in 'coming out' openly about the issue did not stop him becoming a catalyst who began cricket's long argument with Apartheid, which had been aired too as a result of the publication of a best-selling book called *Naught for Your Comfort*[19]. Its author, Father Trevor Huddleston, had been a priest in Sophiatown near Johannesburg and his dauntless work with its black community and support for the African National Congress had made him a legend in South Africa and provoked an eventual recall by his religious order, the Community of Resurrection in 1955. In his book he wrote passionately of 'the irrational madness' of white South Africa. The *News Chronicle* article pitched Sheppard into the full force of the debate about South Africa, and his detachment from other political issues gave him a powerful and resonant moral authority, despite his reluctance to exploit it. Even in the context of this apparent reticence, South African papers like *The Drum* praised Sheppard for a refusal to play in 'racially dominated cricket', and in his autobiography he describes the contents of another newspaper story published in Johannesburg: 'It said that the team on the way to South Africa had each been given a copy of Father Huddleston's book *Naught For Your Comfort*, and had dropped them over the side of the ship at dead of night, while I had not been selected because I would not give an undertaking not to talk politics on the tour'. However, involuntarily, and with what assistance from apocryphal stories, Sheppard the Old Trafford centurion was provoking debate about the most serious moral and political question in world cricket, which touched keenly on the whole future of the southern extreme of the African continent which had been so recently and disastrously invaded at its northern limits by British and French armed forces.

Thinking about all this now, on the very day that one millenium passes into another and four and a half decades separate now-times from faded boyish memories, I read the cricket reports of the current England tour of a post-Apartheid South Africa, albeit against a South African team still virtually all white and only very slowly shifting from its old exclusive profile. The captain of the weak and floundering England team who has just scored a brave century at Durban is not the product of a public school, an Oxford or Cambridge old boy or the son of a rich or propertied family. He is a black young man from the streets where East London meets the Essex suburbs, and his name is Nasser.

## REFERENCES

1 *The Times* (1 August 1956)

2 *The Daily Express* (1 August 1956)

3 Denzil Batchelor, *The Picture Post Book of the Tests* (London, 1956)

4 Richie Benaud, *Antyhing But An Autobiography* (London, 1998)

5 Quoted in W. Scott Lucas, *Divided We Stand: Britain, the US amd the Suez Crisis* (London, 1991)

6 Ibid. I am in debt to the author for this and the following quotations.

7 Ibid.

8 John Pilger, *A Secret Country* (London, 1989)

9 *Punch* (1 August 1956)

10 *Punch* (15 August 1956)

11 Scott Lucas, *Divided We Stand: Britain, the US and the Suez Crisis* (London, 1991)

12 Ibid.

13 Ibid.

14 *Observer* (4 November 1956)

15 Ibid.

16 Roy Fullick and Geoffrey Powell, *Suez: The Double War* (London, 1979)

17 Albert Hourani, *A History of the Arab Peoples* (London, 1991)

18 David Sheppard, *Parson's Pitch* (London, 1964)

19 Trevor Huddleston, *Naught For Your Comfort* (London, 1956)

# 10.

# CRICKET IN PRINT
## Book reviews, 1994-2000

Mike Marqusee:
## Anyone But England
(*Morning Star*, 1 July 1994)

*'ANYONE BUT ENGLAND'*, written by 'deracinated' American Jew Mike Marqusee who lives in England, is probably the second best book on cricket that I have read. The best one, CLR James' *Beyond a Boundary*, is also written by a Marxist from the Americas and is also republished this summer, by Serpent's Tail.

Recalling James' work, Marqusee writes: 'For 200 years, nation and market have nurtured and guided, pummelled and cudgelled cricket. Often they have squabbled over it. And sometimes, gloriously, cricket has burst the boundaries they try to impose on it.'

Perhaps only a non-Englishman could conclude so decisively and with such objective dispassioned truth, that the cultural tailors of the nation's powerful ruling-class would persistently use cricket to clothe their own ugly truth as a 'tell-tale sign of English capital's perennial need to seek a noble rationale for its beastliness.'

But such judgements do not arise from a superficial view of this most complex and unpredictable of sports. Marqusee has immersed himself in cricket and this book is a result of an enormous exercise of assimilating a sporting culture without absorbing an accompanying bias and subjective national cultural value. This is what makes his book so unique, the depth of his understanding of the beauty of the action of cricket, 'the delicacy of its arcane, specialised skills' which, as he grew to love cricket, 'took my breath away.' He writes movingly about both the dancers and the dance, and how this white-flanelled ritual drew him against his will 'ever deeper into English life.'

Yet it is the symbolism of English cricket that fascinates him too, its emblematic quality that invokes a system and its heraldry – 'the parallel between the malaise of English cricket and the economic and social malaise of the country itself' during an era when global prestige and an empire have been replaced by slogans of supremacy, an empty materialism and a racism born of anxiety and national fear.

This is a book that the ruling cricket elite, 'still a faithful mirror of the country's ruling class' – will not find endearing. But it speaks with the same emphasis of the young cricketers who live in the inner city and whom, every day, I see running from their classes to lunchtime cricket practice with a ball and bat in their hands.

These boys – and some girls too – who are the underclass of cricket, young Pakistanis and Caribbean youth who bat and bowl amidst concrete and tar in northern English cities and who are virtually ignored by the governing interests of the national game. Their time is coming, their energy and talent will break through just like it has done in Barbados, Trinidad and Guyana and just like it will in Crossroads and Soweto, carrying with it the energy and brain of their community and class.

Marqusee's history of English cricket's relationship with South Africa and Pakistan, his impressive vindication of the success of the cricket played by Englishwomen and his chronicling of England's humbling cricketing encounter with the Caribbean, also contribute to the power of his book.

Among books of the world of sport, there are few which also express the sport of the world in all its representation of real life and struggle. *Anyone But England* is one, a commentary of our times as well as our runs.

Timothy Arlott:
# John Arlott; A Memoir
(Race and Class, April 1994)

Last summer in Sheffield, the great Caribbean cricketer, Gordon Greenidge of Barbados, a veteran of over two decades of international cricket, visited our school and spoke to a group of our students about his life and career. One of the young cricket enthusiasts asked him how he had started in major cricket. He said that he had been introduced to county level and encouraged to achieve at it by John Arlott, the nonpareil of cricket commentators – whom Greenidge described as 'the Shakespeare of cricket'. Over a quarter of a century ago, in a small Caribbean island where I was teaching, I met a man at work in his clifftop field as I was out walking early one morning in the countryside. He stopped me and we talked. Where was I from, he asked. England, I replied. 'Ah England!' he exclaimed, 'and how is John Arlott?' For me, thousands of miles away from the old radio set in our front room at home, here was its proof writ large – and here was the fame of a voice.

It may seem incredible that a remembrance of a cricket commentator, the son of a cemetery attendant from Hampshire and owner of a bucolic dialect and a poetic facility for describing the processes and settings of the English summer game – a game which became a sphere of black excellence and spur towards nationhood – should be invoked all over the world where cricket is played. But millions came to the game through his unforgettable commentaries, and wondrously evocative descriptions. He made a sport into a poem, and to its players he gave the personalities of characters from a rambling rural novel.

But he was much more, and the biography written by his son, Timothy Arlott, gives a rounded picture of a man of intense generosity yet sometimes blinding self-will, but also of committed and loyal principle.

In 1948 Arlott was travelling as a radio journalist with the England cricket team through South Africa. The tour coincided with the election victory of the National Party led by Malan, which swept the Smuts United Party government from power and proceeded to build the edifice of the apartheid state. On election night, the windscreen of Arlott's car was covered by the spit of National Party supporters, and the visits he later made to the townships around Johannesburg filled him with a loathing for South African racist government and the apartheid system for the rest of his life. It needs to be remembered that during this pre-Sharpeville period the mass of the British public had no real pictures of the oppression of black people in South Africa, although in the empire of their subconscious it must have been present. As a cricket-mad schoolboy in the late 50s I can remember reading *Cricket in the Blood*, the autobiography of Dudley Nourse, ex-captain of the South African team, which was all-white – and to people like me at the time, unquestioningly so. And everything was white in Nourse's book, black people weren't even mentioned. The reader would have imagined, as I did, a white English-speaking land, full of tough yet chivalrous cricketing farmers with their tanned, manly sons.

Thus, Arlott's intervention exposing South Africa's racism, and the effect it had on its black and mixed-race population, was well founded and all the more effective due to his international reputation. His championing of the Cape Town, classified 'coloured' cricketer, Basil D'Oliveira, whom Arlott helped to bring to England in 1960 to play as a professional in the Lancashire League, finally resulted in the severing of cricketing links between England and South Africa – and later South Africa's isolation from world cricket – when the apartheid sporting authorities refused to accept D'Oliveira as a member of the English touring party to South Africa in 1968. Arlott's own steadfast refusal to commentate on matches involving South Africa on the projected 1970 tour to England also created world wide publicity about and pressure upon the apartheid state. During a televised debate at the Cambridge University Union, 'That politics should not intrude upon sporting contacts', Arlott's humanism beamed out across the world: 'Mr President sir, anyone who cares to support this motion will not exclude politics from sport but will in fact be attempting to exclude sport from life.' As Ian Wooldridge, cricket correspondent of the right-wing *Daily Mail,* conceded: 'He won the day not only with sane persuasion, but with a faultless flow of English so beautiful in its construction that you could almost hear the commas and semi-colons fall into place.' It was a victory for the language of the air, the global voice of Arlott.

For if it is by his voice that millions will remember him, his son's book of his father's life is, as well as being brave, critical and lovingly and honestly wrought, a story of pain and loss within a lifelong appreciation of what many hold to be the most generous and epic of games. The death of a son and a wife-companion while in the heart of his fame was concealed from all those who listened intently to him and sat next to him in their imaginations while he talked to them from the Oval, Trent Bridge, Lords, Old Trafford or Headingley. Timothy Arlott's memoir also recounts his father's unhappiness and the loneliness of his last years, spent on the Channel Island of Alderney. For this book is also the story of a particular generation, a generation of lost Englishmen like Arlott, liberal and freethinking in their individual minds and generous in their individual spirits, yet blocked in themselves from shifting that individual humanism towards collective solutions and the economics of equity.

But what a voice, what use of words! And the world – the ex-Empire world of bat, ball and stumps – will never know its like.

Michael Manley:
# A History of West Indies Cricket
*and*
Roy Goble and Bridgette Lawrence:
# The Complete Record of West Indian Test Cricketers
*(Morning Star*, 22 September 1995)

Since ex-Prime Minister of Jamaica Michael Manley first wrote his *History of West Indies Cricket* in 1988, much has happened on and off the Caribbean field. Great and stalwart players have gone. Now there is no Richards or Greenidge, no Marshall or Haynes to wear the purple cap or the crest of palm tree, rock, ocean and stars. Ambrose has come, Lara has come, but the old invincibility is more fragile, with inter-island rivalry more of a divisive issue than it has been for many years and the task of enthusing Caribbean youth with a love of cricket, in the face of an overwhelming Yankee culture, is a new and challenging problem.

Manley's story of sport as history is an epic one and his own political leadership in Jamaica during the `70s, with the years of US interventionist threat and reality at their most intense, were also the most successful and defiant years of West Indies cricket, culminating in the 1984 "blackwash" of England.

The additional chapters of the revised edition centre around the achievements and cricket personalities of two very differently heroic figures of Caribbean cricket. For the last decade meant the swan-song of Viv Richards, "the Lion Heart", as Manley depicts him, looking like "some great African chief of a warrior tribe" – and loyal to the people of Africa in his rejection of apartheid and its rands.

He is described as "the most famous personality and the most feared cricketer" of his epoch, with his very gait on the way to the wicket "a declaration of war soon to be followed by war itself." It is as if Richards, on returning to the pavilion, passed Lara coming to start his innings.

For he is the other monumental figure of Manley's revisions, with 375 now a deeply charged and symbolic number through the islands and on to Guyana. And as Caribbean cricket "had become an activity inextricably bound up with the self-esteem of an entire people", Lara's excellence became the excellence of a people's will and renascent energies.

Manley writes as a lover of cricket, but more so as a lover of his Caribbean, its achievements and dreams. His book is about issues beyond cricket, yet cricket is his organ of hope. As he declares toward the end of this fine and dignified story, "Perhaps one day the people of the Caribbean will do more than admire their cricket team. They might even seek to emulate its success by discovering for themselves the unity which is its secret."

Another inspiring reference book of West Indies cricket is Bridgette Lawrence and Roy Goble's *Complete Record of West Indian Test Cricketers*. Beautifully produced, bursting with biographies and evocative photographs of every player to have represented the West Indies, it is as a tribute to the upsetters of this imperial game, brought as it was to the islands by Nelson's seamen and generations of slaveowners and plantocrats, grasped and transformed to become a moving tableau of regional pride and anti-imperialism. "The West Indian Hall of Fame bulges with names whose feats on the field have become a part of cricketing folklore," writes Lawrence in her introduction, and so does her book – with grace, power and conviction, detailing how the "underdogs" of world cricket became its masters.

There are new forces too, in and beyond the islands. Gary Sobers's preface emphasises the significant new contributions of cricketers from the smaller islands – from Antigua, Nevis, St Vincent and Grenada for example and a short, but fascinating section offers portraits of Caribbean-born players who have represented England – from Malcolm to Slack, from Small to De Freitas.

Sport and scholarship here, proud and detailed – inspiring and emblematic.

Hilary McD Beckles (ed):
# Liberation Cricket
(*Morning Star*, 18 September 1995)

At the Cave Hill campus of the University of the West Indies in Barbados, there is now a well-established course in the History of West Indies Cricket since 1820. This has been organised by the Professor of History, Hilary McD Beckles – who, as well as being a luminous historian of the anti-slavery movements in the Caribbean and the author of *Natural Rebels*, a study of Barbadian women who resisted slavery – is a cricket enthusiast and scholar of its vibrant and momentous history within his region.

*Liberation Cricket* is an essential text for Beckles's course and is also a pathbreaking book toward an understanding that popular sport not only symbolised and expresses the movements and aspirations of ordinary people throughout the world, but, more than this – it is their struggle.

Inspired by CLR James's seminal work on the Caribbean and its cricketers, *Beyond a Boundary*, the authors of the many articles comprising *Liberation Cricket* manifest his much-quoted axiom: "What do they know of cricket who only cricket know?" As co-editor, Brian Stoddart concludes, James's theme is still ripe: "The contours of the modern game as played and conveyed by Caribbean people are still essentially about struggle in one form or another." For the imperial game, which was planted in the Caribbean islands alongside sugar, slavery, the Anglican Church and the English language, took some prising away from the colonial and pale-skinned elite, to be transformed by the anti-colonial genius of Caribbean cricket from Constantine and Headley onward to Sobers, Kanhai, Richards and the great battery of pace bowling.

There are certain incidents and moments to which these essays continually return – these are turning points, conjunctions in Caribbean history in which cricket signalled bursts of change. There was the "victory Test match" at Lord's in 1950 when Caribbean cricket first broke through the boundaries of the colonising power at their very conjunction of imperial leisure. There was the bottle-throwing incident on the 1953-4 MCC tour by the crowd at Georgetown, Guyana, which came hot on the heels of the British invasion of "British Guiana" and the dismissal and arrest of Cheddi Jagan and his People's Progressive Party government. There was the struggle that was waged by James and thousands of other Caribbean people to ensure that the racist tradition of white captains of the West Indies side ended and the true creative strength of West Indian cricket – in the person of Frank Worrell – was allowed to prevail with the appointment, at last, of a black leader.

There is a spectrum of perspectives on the Caribbean game in this fine and fascinating book, including essays in the links between cricket and West Indian literature, the role of the "crowd", the contribution of women cricketers and a number of analyses of James's insights. It makes you wish very much that you, too, were a student on this pioneering course at Cave Hill.

It also turns your mind to all sport. Did you watch the semi-final of the Rugby World Cup in Johannesburg earlier this summer, where one of the teams was a South African side with but one black player? Do you recall how the start was delayed by a torrential downpour and a team of black women with giant brooms moved into action to sweep away the pools of water?

What did that tell us? That the blacks are still sweeping while the whites are still playing? Or is this merely the residue of apartheid and white power being swept away too?

Edward Griffiths:
## Kepler: The Biography
(*Morning Star*, 8 July 1994)

This is the story of the cricketing life of Kepler Wessels, a man, we are told by the Zimbabwe-born white South African journalist Edward Griffiths, who has 'stood his ground, gutsed it out … and prevailed',

In his preface, Wessels's frequently hagiographic biographer tells us that he 'faced the barrier of race' and that his life is an example that 'no matter how dark the night, no matter how great the obstacle, guts can carry you through'.

In a country with so grotesque a history of racism as South Africa, the uninformed reader may well think that this is the story of a brave sportsman who spent his life struggling against the apartheid system – described by Griffiths as 'misguided' – for there are many, many of them in the townships and rural areas of South Africa.

But not so. This is the story of sporting opportunism at its most intense, dressed up as Boys' Own heroism.

Kepler Wessels came to prominence as an Afrikaans-speaking South African in the mid-1970s, when the struggle against apartheid was at its zenith. He is a contemporary of those brave, young, black South Africans who were shot down in their hundreds in Soweto. When he saw that there was no future for him in international cricket as a South African – 'he was all padded up with nowhere to go,' writes Griffiths – he emigrated to Sydney as a part of the Kerry Packer money-making enterprise, became an Australian and represented Australia in 24 Test matches. Suddenly, 'opportunity was everywhere. He would fight on. The struggle would continue'.

This crude parody of one of the most popular and determined slogans of the southern African liberation movement, is, in fact, a commentary upon Wessels's next move – to join an Australian 'rebel' tour of South Africa. He returned to his birthplace for rands – rather than runs – galore. Griffiths describes all this in terms of unmitigated praise. 'Wessels had only ever been a gutsy cricketer giving it all for his country'. Which country? And was it giving … or was it taking?

All this recounting of cricketing events is described by Griffiths as 'constructive history', which 'can't be viewed through binoculars and without taking into account the views and circumstances at the time'.

Exactly! The reader concludes, the 'views and circumstances' of South Africa's struggling black majority.

Wessels stayed on in the country of his birth, became captain of Eastern Province and subsequently captain of a South African cricket team at last readmitted into world Test cricket – with Wessels, according to Griffiths, the man 'who successfully led South Africa in from the cold'. I suppose that this book will be widely justified and defended as a part of the process and literature of national 'reconciliation'.

Yet in this vital stabilising period in South Africa, surely truth must never be the loser.

The notion that Wessels and other cricketing mercenaries 'never moved anywhere because of money', or that 'he joined two rebel squads because there was nothing else to do' are at the least implausible, at the most a blatantly false rewriting of cultural history.

South Africa was brought back into the sporting arena by the struggle and achievement of its people – predominantly black – who launched wave after wave of resistance against the inhumanity and fascist dictatorship of the apartheid system and those who directly benefited from it. That included its oppressed cricketers, banned from smart Test match grounds, consigned to bare, ashen pitches on the wasted ground of the townships, fighting for resources and recognition with every run scored and every wicket taken.

Let us at least read of the life of privileged cricketers like Kepler Wessels in that true and naked context.

Mike Proctor:

# South Africa: The years of isolation and the return to international cricket

(*Morning Star*, 14 October 1994)

When Devon Malcolm told South African fast bowler Fanie de Villiers, 'You're history!' after the latter had smashed his batting helmet in the last Test match, and then proceeded to demolish the South African batting with his crushing 9-57, the Jamaican-born and Sheffield-bred paceman's words were pregnant with meaning. Now some of that meaning comes out clearly in Mike Procter's book: *South Africa: the years of isolation and the return to international cricket*.

Procter was a world-class all-rounder whose best years of international cricket were lost to the curse of apartheid. His Test career ended at the age of 23 when South Africa was expelled from world cricket. Now returned to the mainstream as the manager of the post-apartheid South African team, his book is a fascinating piece of sporting history.

Firstly, Procter is reflective and self-critical about the years of isolation. He writes: 'I had been brainwashed as a boy. I assumed apartheid was the right thing, simply because it was in place and we whites seemed happy'. Then in April 1971, with a group of other white South African players, Procter had walked off the field at Newlands Cricket Ground in Cape Town, as a protest against the apartheid government refusing to include two 'non-whites' in the Test team. He now concedes that it took the sporting boycott and isolation 'to make us understand what had to be done'. He and others like Ali Bacher worked hard within the cricket infrastructures to struggle toward multiracial cricket, but much of this activity was hermetic, sealed off from the political struggle and the ANC commitment to the boycott. It was as if cricket could exist alone, outside politics.

Procter writes: 'South Africa still had intense political problems, with the government wielding the big stick at various stages – but what could we sportsmen do about that?' Ask Steve Tshwete, cricketer and ANC militant who spent 15 years on Robben Island with Mandela and who eventually negotiated South Africa back into the international cricket arena.

Procter's book is full of commitment to, and enthusiasm for, a multiracial cricket future for South Africa, based upon a revolution of coaching and resources for the townships. It is the success, large-scale resourcing and power of such initiatives at the school and community level that will make Devon's strong words come true.

Alistair McLellan:

## The Enemy Within

(*Morning Star*, 14 October 1994)

To call a book about the impact of overseas players on English cricket *The Enemy Within* is strangely provocative for what is a well-written and carefully researched work. Yet Thatcher's words about striking mineworkers truly reflects the attitude of many in the cricket establishment about foreign – predominantly black – cricketers playing in the county circuit. Alistair

McLellan's statistics demonstrate that 'the decline of England as a cricketing power coincided with the number of overseas players in county cricket reaching its peak'.

This is hardly surprising, as Caribbean, Pakistani or New Zealand players like Richards, Marshall, Imran Khan or Hadlee sharpened their already mature skills on the English county game and became even more accomplished. But the boot was on the other foot too – a whole generation of world-class overseas players also revealed their weaknesses as well as their strengths to English players and pundits.

This should have improved the English performance too. But it didn't – largely because the talent and motivation of the emergent cricket nations was more determined and often rooted in their surging ambition to defeat the old colonial power.

McLellan's book is at its best when describing the real situations faced by foreign cricketers in England – such as what he calls 'Somerset's Greek tragedy' and the brutal treatment meted to Garner and Richards when their contracts were terminated. And while recounting the times of the early overseas players, McLellan tells of the experience of the pioneering CA Olivierre from the Caribbean island of St Vincent. While playing for Derbyshire against Essex in 1904 he was involved in a run-chase with a racist batting partner. Olivierre was determined to reach a century, his team-mate was equally determined to deny him one, their antagonisms boiling up as they ran between the wickets to win the game.

Something of an apt parable for one side of the life of the black arrivant worker in England, cricket or otherwise.

Bridgette Lawrence:

# Masterclass: The Biography of George Headley

*and*

Brian Lara with Brian Scovell:

## Beating the Field

(*Morning Star*, 25 August 1995)

The publication of the lives of two great Caribbean batsmen – one a pathmaking legend, the other a contemporary genius – gives the opportunity to compare and assess their huge contribution to world cricket. Just as Toussaint L'Ouverture was called a 'Black Spartacus' or CLR James a 'Black Plato', so in his lifetime, George Headley, born 1909, the Jamaican who, along with his Trinidadian confrere, Learie Constantine, carried West Indian cricket on his slight shoulders in the years before World War II, was dubbed the 'Black Bradman'. Definitions were made by white colonial 'civilisation', yet Headley's achievements, which are so clearly set down in Bridgette Lawrence's beautifully cogent and telling little book, surpassed and redefined them. Lawrence is an accomplished scholar of people's sport. Her books on Caribbean cricket, which include a life of Roland Butcher, England's first Caribbean-born international, have made a particularly invaluable mark in developing a broader understanding of the game.

In her portrayal of Headley, she describes his early Isthmian years playing baseball, the son of a migrant canal construction worker in Panama from Barbados and a Jamaican mother. His struggle as a black cricketer playing a sport that was controlled and defined by colonial whites – his first meeting with Constantine was when, in 1930 as black West Indies team members, they shared a bed in accommodation offered to them in British Guiana – his brilliance throughout the `30s, including a century in each innings in both the Caribbean and at Lord's and his enormous popularity as a symbol of rising Jamaican nationhood and his period as national cricket coach in Nigeria – are told by Lawrence with a combination of narrative eloquence and use of some evocative photographs and documents from Headley's life and times.

A long overdue recognition for a luminous life in sport is *Masterclass* and, compared to it, *Beating the Field*, which is ghostwritten by a 25-year-old cricketer, may seem to be more than a little previous.

But there is nothing premature about the substance and talent of Brian Lara's achievement. The young Trinidadian sees his direct forebears as the 'West Indian labourers' who 'wanted to be different in their approach to the game from the people who oppressed them, so they were much more aggressive, using their physical strength and gift of co-ordination between hand and eye to strike the ball great distances'. He adds: 'West Indian cricket will always be aggressive and exciting because as people we do not like being restricted'.

Anyone who has studied Lara's batting art will see the acuity of these words. The high backlift is as the lifting of a staff, the follow through as the ball fires toward the offside boundary is as the raising of a sceptre. It is dance and power, a mode of beauty that also inspires a social emulation.

*Beating the Field* could be much more than the conventional ghostwritten sporting biography, for Lara's symbolic importance may yet go beyond his extraordinary feats as a cricketer. Between two futures, the devil or humanity, he poses as a city gent in bowler and pinstripes at the Tower Hotel for a deal struck with a leading investment house. Then he travels to South Africa to coach young township cricketers. Elemental choices for Lara indeed, with huge chasms separating them, yet with the disarming and modest tone that characterises much of his opinion in this revealing, if carefully edited, self-portrait, he declares in the most optimistic of stances: 'Although walking down the street in London and being recognised can be a good feeling, walking through Soweto and considered a hero felt a lot better and meant more to me'.

Cricket, but more than cricket here.

Mike Marqusee:

# War Minus the Shooting

(*Morning Star*, 8 November 1996)

On the front cover of this extraordinarily adroit and finely written book is a photograph which is piercing in its raw symbolism. The Sri Lankan batsman, Aravinda de Silva – a principal player in his country's against-the-odds victory of the 1996 cricket World Cup – brandishes his giant winner's cheque under the floodlights of Lahore's stadium, between two heavily armed Pakistani soldiers.

The image is sharply emblematic, for the centrepiece of the giant cheque is also the theme around which Mike Marqusee's book orbits. For it is a book about an American's deep and unleashed love for cricket and those who play and watch it, certainly, but its brilliance lies in the way that it pitches the culture of cricket within the burgeoning superstructure of a rampaging, unchecked capitalism and its operations in its own newfoundland of South Asia. 'Cricket', writes Marqusee, 'whose sole purpose is the pleasure it can give players and spectators, was being parcelled out and auctioned off, like British Rail'.

For the writer's huge commitment is to the ordinary people who play and watch the game worldwide. There, in India, Pakistan and Sri Lanka, they were being sucked into a war of capital, where whoever won the cup, it was the multinationals – Coca-Cola, Pepsi, Fuji, Visa, Reebok, Sony Mastercard, Shell and Oncida, plus the giant satellite television corporations – that were the most prominent players, leaving the ordinary spectators, as one official put it, 'only there to create the atmosphere'.

*War Minus the Shooting* works powerfully as a travel narrative. It was the nature of the tournament that the venues were long distances apart, scattered in stadia across the three countries, from Colombo to Calcutta to Karachi. The author flies and hustles his way between these domes of cricket, always ready to reshape his understanding of the great landmass and its people: 'Every day there is a school day; I am always learning'. He is a true spectator of cricketing peoples and the systems which warp and dehumanise them, as well as their generosity and culture in the 'democratic domain, where cricket and its meanings are shared and shaped by multitudes'. And cricket is their game, despite its disfigurement by commerce and nationalism and the £4,000 profits-a-ball made by those corporations which ride it.

There is Delhi and its VIP culture, where, after the local power-brokers and society posers have had their pick of the tickets, only a few hundred are left to go on sale and the police, swinging their *lathis* 'play polo' with the ordinary and true cricket lovers. Or Bombay, 'a city of dreams, where the stuff of dreams is cricket'. Marqusee's passion and indignation find their particular subject in the twisted alliance that he continually encounters between capital and resurgent nationalism. For, in the World Cup, a 'carnival of globalisation' has 'turned into an orgy of nationalism'. This is a nationalism nurtured by the global economy, where the same multinationals produce stirring chauvinist slogans to market their products in two neighbouring nations competing in the most volatile of sporting encounters, and where their soldiers are shooting at each other across the Kashmir frontiers.

For cricket, racked with contradiction and divide, is Marqusee's living metaphor, yet his passion too. At its best, it fosters and empowers internationalism – as in the solidarity match played in Sri Lanka between a national team and players – Pakistanis and Indians, Muslims and Hindus – all opposed to the boycott of Sri Lankan venues by the Australian and West Indian teams who were fearful of terrorist attacks. For, beyond the exposures and lucid illustrations of the new imperialism at work in the sport which grew from the old imperialism and has been transformed by those peoples over which it ruled, Marqusee's book is a declaration of the internationalism of cricket and its true players and followers – an internationalism which 'places no restrictions on your growth. It has no limits'.

This is sport as the blood of life, its people, its systems, its degradations, its triumphs – not a few separate cells in isolation but the whole of the body, flesh, mind and politic.

Don Oslear and Jack Bannister:
# Tampering With Cricket
(*Hit Racism for Six*, Summer 1996)

Both the cover and the time of publication of *Tampering with Cricket* reveal the book's true purpose.

The front of the dust jacket shows the brown-skinned arm of a flannelled cricketer beside the reddened stain on the crotch of his trousers. His hand holds a ball, the index finger appears to be scratching its leather surface. Ah! It must be a Pakistani fast bowler, deduces the English reader, particularly as this summer will be Pakistan's first cricketing visit since 1992 and the 'ball tampering' series.

The anonymous figure – cropped at the chest, headless and unidentifiable – adds a suggestion of menace. When you turn the book over you recognise the familiar figure (this time including the face) of England captain Mike Atherton, concentrating too on changing the surface of a cricket ball, as he did on 23 July 1994 during the Lord's Test against South Africa – at first denying it and later admitting that he had a pocketful of dust concealed to 'age' the ball. Yet according to the theme on the front cover and the context of the book's publication (a few weeks before the arrival of the Pakistanis), 'tampering' is definitely a foreign blight on cricket, something Asian and fundamentally non-English and not-cricket, a Pakistani curse upon the game. Thus, despite much of its content focusing on other abuses of cricket and its authorities, the book's publication and publicity profile must be synchronised to coincide with the arrival of Waqar, Wasim et al – to set the tabloid hounds baying.

For in Oslear and Bannister's book we find the conventional caricatures: Pakistani cricketers 'are volatile by nature', they have a 'naturally volatile character', a temperament which suits a people coming from such a country, 'bedevilled by instability'. But the authors' carping on this theme of 'volatility' and its attribution to some kind of natural or biological function takes the ethos of the book back to the infamous Robert Henderson article in *Wisden Cricket Monthly* and the question posed in its title: 'Is it in the Blood?' Oslear and Bannister also indulge in the same bogus assumptions of scientific racism, resorting to genetic myth and stereotype.

In opposition to those Asiatic elements who create 'the festering sore of ball tampering' there is the upright and incorruptible Don Oslear, who umpired during that 1992 England versus Pakistan series when the issue first came to national and international prominence. Of course, different versions of this controversy have been going on for decades. I can remember as a boy watching the black and white television images of Tony Lock and Jim Laker rubbing new balls ferociously into the dust around the bowling crease to better their spinners' grip and make the ball more liable to turn, and even further back Keith Miller, the Australian darling of the Brylcreem ads, using his hair grease to put an unnaturally keen shine on the oldest and most battered of balls.

Oslear and Bannister themselves quote the tampering antics of the two Pringles – Derek of Essex and Chris of New Zealand, and their open admissions of developing the technique. Yet somehow the reader is still left with the idea that this is largely a Pakistani habit generated originally by bowlers such as Sarfraz and Imran. The truth of the matter is that in 1992 Wasim Akram and Waqar Younis were the foremost fast bowlers of the world. They were simply the best, and they exploited the skills of reverse swing and the old ball with more accuracy and effectiveness than any other bowlers in the world. It was their brilliance that gained them wickets, their speed, full length and consistent direction combined with an aptitude for using the old ball which they had learned and perfected through necessity, on the unhelpful and flat pitches of their own country. Thus their cricket and its success was a produce of their culture: some of those who could not match it could only label it a product of cheating.

It is a shame that the positive sections of *Tampering with Cricket* are demeaned by ugly attitudes and Oslear's apparent determination to settle old scores. Some of the book's assertions and stereotypes are like those of the old colonial judges, who sat on the bench rather than stood in the middle in the old territories of Empire: riddled with comments and judgements on the habits of those subjects from the 'subcontinent' or the manners of those with, for example, 'a Leeward Islands upbringing' who swear on the cricket pitch. For the book reveals much about the seamier sides of world professional cricket: the fixing of games, the smears of bribery, the power of gambling syndicates in Dubai and Bombay, the fudging of remedial measures to clean up the international game by cricket authorities – down to the shameful act of the Test and County Cricket Board in forcing Oslear's early retirement when his forthrightness provoked too many complexities for them to handle.

*Tampering with Cricket* touches upon much that besmirches the game. However, it also exemplifies a form of racism and stereotyping that despoils English cricket even more profoundly.

Charles Williams:

## Bradman

*and*

Alan Hill:

## Peter May: A Biography

(*Morning Star*, 21 February 1997)

I was brought up in a cricketing culture which dictated that the 'natural enemy' was neither Germany nor France but Australia and every Englishman's prime antagonist was a man slight in body but huge in runs, called Don Bradman. He had retired from the game by the time I was a boy, but his huge reputation hung over world cricket like a brilliant sunset, as Hutton and Harvey, Compton and Lindwall, Miller and Trueman still batted and bowled on in his indelible shadow.

In his biography, Charles Williams or Lord Williams of Elvel – I remember him as C C P Williams, an Oxford University amateur who played a few seasons for Essex in the mid-1950s – sees Bradman as an Australian icon, a symbol of the country's emergent nationhood in the years between two wars. For simply the name of this carpenter's son from Bowral, in the rural hinterland of New South Wales – whose ancestors came from a village in Suffolk – stirred awe in the hearts of his cricketing contemporaries all over the world. One of Nelson Mandela's first questions upon his release was whether Don Bradman was still alive. And the infamous 'Bodyline' series of test matches in 1932-33, which provoked such Anglo-Australian dissonance, was directly caused by the England captain Jardine's obsession with dealing with Bradman's batting genius, and getting 'the Australian bastards on the run'. All this was cricket, but much more too. And the very positive quality of William's account is that he deals with the 'Bradmania' as much as Bradman himself.

That a cricketer could inspire so much on-the-pitch malice by his brilliance and see that transformed to become a virtual idolisation during his final tour of England in 1948 is a story well told by Williams. For within the history of the game, no other cricketer has matched Bradman's run-getting achievement. A test average of 99 and a century on every third walk to the wicket in first-class games is still a breathless career feat. Williams seeks too to show the pressures besetting this 'Australian hero' – in particular the hostility to him, as a New South Wales protestant, from the Irish Catholic cricketing forces of Melbourne in the persons of powerful team-mates like Bill O'Reilly, Jack Fingleton and Stan McCabe.

A predictable and well-rehearsed tale of patriotic heroes and republican villains this, but at least Williams sees cricket for what it is beyond the contest on the pitch – as a social and political engagement played out in the theatre of ideas and their economic causes. And in this, Don Bradman was one of the great symbols and begetters of national pride and cultural identity.

Alan Hill's biography of Peter May, the most successful post-war English batsman, is an altogether slighter book, which, given the power of its subject, could have been a much richer story. For unlike Bradman, who was never coached as a boy and learned his batting by throwing a golf ball against his backyard wall and hitting the rebound with a stump, P.B.H. May was a public school cricketing prodigy, whose route to the England captaincy was a privileged journey via Charterhouse and its intensive coaching, Cambridge and Surrey. Here was a player described by his biographer as one 'who scattered his stardust on the field, but was rooted in detachment off it'.

Hill's account is much more personal, less concerned with social and cultural context, much more orthodox in its virtual hagiographical presentation and thus much less pregnant with meaning than Williams. Yet May was a transitional figure of his age, a 'golden amateur' when such a status was in fast decline, a conservative, diffident figure whose captaincy success was largely built on the outstanding bowlers he had at his command – Trueman, Statham, Lock, Wardle – and the unsurpassable phenomenon of Jim Laker's off-spin which found its apogee against Australia in the 1956 Old Trafford test.

The contrast between these two biographies is sharply made in their covers. May resplendent in his Surrey blazer and aristocratic badge, is painted alone and emblematic before the Oval skyline; Bradman is picked out returning from the wicket enveloped by thousands of admiring inter-war Australians – a man holding a bat and the dreams of a nation, taking on its far away colonisers.

Brian Stoddart and A.P. Sandiford:
## The Imperial Game
(*Morning Star*, 9 April 1999)

The front cover of *The Imperial Game* – a historical study of 'cricket, culture and society' edited by two scholars of sport, Brian Stoddart and A.P. Sandiford – sports a most emblematic painting of a cricket match being played on Singapore's Padang in 1851. All the imperial components are there. Members of the colonial aristocracy, trussed up in Victorian jackets and top hats, ride around the boundary in carriages and groomed white horses. A red-uniformed, black imperial soldier, appears to be 'pacifying' an argument between a group of local men in front of them and, in the background, before the elegant walls of some pillared, British-style stately houses, a game of cricket, serene and majesterial, is in progress. That cricket woven into the very fabric of British imperialism in its mission all over the world has rarely been more clearly expressed. And this book, for example, becomes the painting's commentary and exegesis.

But cricket this century has also been a story of the history of anti-imperialism – an expression of the colonised human's ability and will to use those cultural forms most intimate and precious to the coloniser – indeed, the very cultural flesh and mind of the coloniser - not only to emulate but also to resist, subvert, create betterment and to overcome. Think of the images of Bradman's phenomenal Australian run-getting for two decades over the English colonial masters, Viv Richards striding to the wicket, his African wristband whirling with the revolutions of his arms and his bat. Waqar's perplexing reverse swing, the Caribbean pace of Hall, Roberts, Holding Marshall and Ambrose, the Sri Lankan joy at holding the World Cup, the struggle and beauty in the Trinidadian words of CLR James in *Beyond A Boundary* and the calypsonian's delight at Lord's in 1950, as Ramadhin and Valentine spun the West Indies to victory before the eyes of the Windrush arrivants.

But, back to *The Imperial Game* which is excellent in both its facts and insights. In his introduction, Sandiford shows how cricket both intersected and paralleled lines of class and race. 'Thus the snobberies which afflicted the game in Victorian England, dividing aristocratic amateur from plebeian professional, reappeared in the racial and ethnic divides bedevilling the sport almost wherever it was taken,' he writes.

Coming home too, in the present gulf between the attention and resources offered to young, predominantly Asian cricketing talent in British inner cities, compared to what is on offer in the suburbs and exclusive schools. No essential change here in a game still wrapped around class and race.

In chapters devoted to the main cricket-playing, ex-colonial nations, the authors offer many sporting revelations. The chapter on South Africa by Christopher Merrett and John Nauright is fascinating, particularly in its telling of the role of powerful industrial and landholding magnates like Sir Abe Bailey, who underwrote cricket development and the most immoral 'moral metaphor and imperial symbol' that also underwrote apartheid. The authors' research also reveals in 1894 a reversal of the 'D'Oliveira affair'. When the British authorities refused to accept the South African selection of 'coloured' pace bowler Krom Hendricks – reputed to be the fastest of his era – for the tour of England, thus laying an early basis of the English worst cricketing nightmare of black fast bowlers.

This is a fine commentary of the centrality of politics and economic and cultural realities in sport, a process forever true and ably expressed by Stoddart in his subliminal last sentences. He writes: 'Cricket everywhere is a produce of its environment, whether in subtle or spectacular form. It is contoured by the social needs of its players and supporters and to read cricket is to read life'.

And if you love the game, read this book too, for it will provoke much reflection and understanding.

## Richie Benaud:
# Anything but an Autobiography
### (*Morning Star*, 6 January 1999)

Every sports lover has a figure who seems to have been there during every phase in their life of sport – from childhood to now. Even today, as I gain some happiness watching the televised highlights of England's long-aspired win at Melbourne, through the tremendous feats of Stewart, Gough and Headley and that catch by Ramprakash – it is presented by Richie Benaud, who seems to have accompanied me all through a life's passion for cricket. Benaud was there, on the losing side for a change, when, as a boy, I watched England regain the Ashes at the Oval in 1953. He was duly Lakered twice at Old Trafford in 1956. He captained Australia in that incredible tied test against Worrell's West Indies in the 1960-61 series. As one of the great Australian all-rounders, he was the first cricketer ever to reach 2,000 runs and 200 wickets in test matches. And, as a TV presenter, he has been giving his wise, erudite and understated commentaries for 35 years. It's quite a life and it's set down in *Anything But An Autobiography* by the descendant of Captain Jean Benaud – the French master of a ship carrying whale oil which arrived in Sydney in 1840 – and the Saville family of farmers from East Anglia.

Celebrated for his insightful and hugely successful captaincy, Benaud was often characterised by English cricket writers as 'crafty, shrewd, tough and merciless' – the epitome of the Australian playing cricket. Yet his book is anything but an exercise in self-glory, swank or a vindication of such caricatured Australian 'virtues'. It is much more a tribute to those who helped and moulded him – his father Lou, himself a talented grade cricketer, playing colleagues like Neil Harvey, Ray Lindwall, Keith Miller and Alan Davidson, cricketing foes like Frank Worrell and Jim Laker – or Ivan James, a dispensing chemist of Tamaru, New Zealand, who gave him the remedy to toughen up his splitting and work-mutilated spinning finger during a 1956 tour, enabling him to carry on bowling his finger spin with outstanding success in the ensuing years.

Bred in New South Wales countryside along the Murrambridgee river where his father was a teacher, Benaud is very conscious of his history – his forebears' experiences of the Depression, the 'yoke of a 'muttonous' diet' and the early cricketing experiences of legendary players like Sam Anderson, an aboriginal pioneer of whom an admirer wrote:

> *They won't care if his skin was black,*
> *Or that he came to them from a drover's shack,*
> *For they judge men, up there, by their deeds they say,*
> *And Sam was champion on his day.*

Although Benaud is very cagey about his politics, his book is the work of a skilled and practised raconteur who has much to tell. In 1975, he was approached to lead a private cricket tour of apartheid South Africa. He laid down strict conditions. Crowds must be allowed to mix freely, all bars must be open to all, officials of any non-white organisation must be able to meet him and every South African team must include three non-white players. These conditions were met by the cricket-desperate authorities. He recalls a brusque meeting with Prime Minister BJ Vorster, who reminded him that all visitors to South Africa 'were expected to conform to the laws of the land'. Benaud replied by saying that, if any of his conditions were not adhered to, he would 'go home and my players would go with me'. Vorster, he declared, spoke by 'verbally poking you in the chest whilst never able to bring himself to catch your eye'.

Perhaps Benaud's most moving reminiscences involve the continuity of Australian cricketing genius. He made his debut in the retirement year of the phenomenal Bradman. He recounts the 1953 advice that was given to him in a Scarborough hotel room by 'Tiger' Bill O'Reilly, the greatest Australian bowler of a previous generation. 'Give the batsman absolutely nothing!' It seemed to sum up the Australian supremacy – and Benaud passed it on to Shane Warne in the '90s and it runs through the blood of the Waughs, the tight line of McGrath and the astute captaincy of Mark Taylor.

Still, as I write this, England celebrate at Melbourne, so there is more than hope for us, even beyond Benaud's wry eyes and generous words.

Hilary McD Beckles:
# The Development of West Indies Cricket (Vols 1 and 2)
(*Morning Star*, 9 April 1999)

The sudden and glorious resurgence of West Indies cricket during the just-completed series against Steve Waugh's Australians seems to have astonished many cricket commentators. However, those who know how close cricket is to the vital well-springs of Caribbean culture will not be surprised. The fractured and Balkanised Caribbean nation has been enduring a regional torment and agony for almost two decades.

The prevailing economic and cultural domination from US multinationals, media giants and drug interests, the repeated depredations of the World Bank and the International Monetary Fund and the imposition of strangulating and anti-democratic structural adjustment packages that send the hopes of entire populations of the islands into reverse, the increasing fragmentation of small island states pressed into subnationalist ideologies, the role of the US-based right-wing churches and fundamentalist sects, the humiliations of a tourist industry thriving upon caricatures of Caribbean culture and reality, the weakening and diminution of erstwhile vigorous and influential left and trade union organisations that fell into the disastrous wake of the implosion of the Grenada revolution and the subsequent invasion ... it has not been an easy epoch for Caribbean progress.

Throughout these years, two institutions in particular have sought to hold aloft the democratic and resilient tradition of Caribbean unity and optimism and, in doing so, have continued to echo Maurice Bishop's visionary cry: 'One Caribbean!' One of these is the region's university – still serving all the English-speaking sub-nations – the University of the West Indies, with its campuses in Jamaica, Trinidad and Barbados – and with programmes in progress in all the other island states. The other – hugely symbolic and signally prestigious – is the West Indies cricket team.

The author of the two luminous volumes of *The Development of West Indies Cricket*, Hilary McD Beckles, knows both these institutions intimately. He is professor of history and a Pro Vice Chancellor at the Jamaica campus and a lifelong cricket lover and student of the game – as a young man in Birmingham, he was on Warwickshire's books for a short time in the early 1970s. He also pioneered a course on Caribbean cricket culture and established the Centre for Cricket Studies at the Barbados campus.

Now, throughout these two finely written and powerfully insightful books, Beckles asserts that West Indian people fused the old Victorian, imperial game as it was originally exposed to them, with 'an intense sense of progressive purpose' and transformed it to a cultural expression of resistance and nationhood, leading up to its contemporary manifestation in the particular talent of Brian Lara, a 'man-child of genius' in an era of globalisation.

The first volume, *The Age of Nationalism*, demonstrates how Caribbean cricketers – and the devotees and crowds who passionately identified with them – progressively democratised, redefined and used the game for their own empowerment during the later years of colonialism and the lasting legacy of colonial racism that was at that system's centre. He argues that the liberal, inclusive influence of the Trinidad-born cricketing aristocrat Sir Pelham Warner, plus the phenomenal talent and nationalist conviction of great cricketers such as Learie Constantine, George Headley, Frank Worrell – and writer/activists such as CLR James, were central to the struggle for Caribbean unity and nationhood.

Beckles – an excellent storyteller himself – tells how, as a boy in Birmingham and recently arrived from Barbados, he remembers a photograph that his friend's Caribbean father had kept of himself on the mantlepiece since 1950, dressed in Tuxedo – hat, gloves and all. He had celebrated the West Indies win at Lord's in 1950 – Ramadhin and Valentine's Test match – by wearing this apparel for a day while he drove buses for the West Midlands Transport Board, so much had the victory affected his pride and consciousness.

Real human stories such as this pepper Beckles's remarkable books. He includes a most moving tribute to the Caribbean's greatest warrior-maroon of cricket, Viv Richards, whose rebellious and patriotic love of Caribbean culture and its African provenances, made him such a formidable and wilful opponent and symbolised the fusion of cricket and popular sovereignty.

In the second volume, *The Age of Globalisation*, Beckles considered the 'new paradigm that is characterised by the privatisation, commodification and global liberalisation of cricket' and personifies Lara as its first hero and 'icon leader'. He describes how this 'age' has provoked, in economic and social terms, a crisis for Caribbean small-island communities, with villages 'inhabited by spiritual despair ... harbouring safe-houses for narcotics, crime and the worst kind of anti-social action'. Cricket has been subjugated in the context of a 'value system antithetical' to the survival strategies of the youth and no longer can act as a transforming social force like it did in the previous era. It has also suffered body blows from European tourism interests. At the 1994 Barbados test match against England, on which Beckles has an illuminating chapter, 80 per cent of those holding tickets – expensive enough commodities – were the travelling English. Local cricket enthusiasts were costed right out. Simultaneously, Caribbean cricket – with its essential regionally unifying emphasis, appears to have outlived its moment and seems like an anachronism, in an historical period of the strife and bickering between subnational island politics, urged on by globalisation's contradictory fragmenting energy.

Yet the same deafening cry of Caribbean unity and progress that rings through the living words of James, Bishop, Rodney, Marley, Marryshow, Lamming, Braithwaite, through the batting, strength and artistry of Headley, Weekes, Richards and Kanhai, the speed force of Wes Hall, Michael Holding and Malcolm Marshall, the spin power of Ramadhin and Gibbs and the all-round genius of Constantine and Sobers – all this was expressed again in the third Test of the just-finished series with the achievements of Lara's marvellous batting and Courtney Walsh's tireless and tenacious bowling. In their victory, they wrote a modern redemption song for Caribbean cricket and instilled a renewed sense of regional oneness and pride wherever Caribbean roots are watered and nurtured.

So there could be no better time to read and ingest Beckles's original and deeply perceptive work – which shows again how sport is more than sport and how cricket, as always, is definitely much more than cricket and replete with all manner of social and political meaning – in the Caribbean, in Essex and in Yorkshire, in Bombay, Sydney and Soweto or anywhere on an English April day, where the pitch of life is rolled out.

Courtney Walsh and Derek Hodgson:

## Courtney: Heart of the Lion

*(Morning Star, 20 July 1999)*

Of the three bowlers who have captured over 400 wickets in test cricket, the achievement of the Jamaican fast bowler Courtney Walsh is probably the most impressive. Whereas, in his test career, Richard Hadlee, the tricenturion of New Zealand, dominated the national team's bowling attacks and had little competition, Walsh's early years in the West Indies team found him alongside a trio of the greatest fast bowlers in cricket history – Michael Holding, Joel Garner and Malcolm Marshall, plus, as the years went along, other powerful pace bowlers like Colin Croft, Patrick Patterson, Ian Bishop and the formidable Curtley Ambrose.

Thus, his 424 test wickets are a tribute to his inexhaustible staying power, as noted by Viv Richards in his foreword to *Courtney: Heart of the Lion*. Richards writes that Walsh is 'an icon of durability, persistence and endless stamina'. His test career goes back to 1984 and involved him playing under various captains, from Clive Lloyd, Viv Richards and Richie Richardson to Desmond Haynes and Brian Lara. And, in the spaces between these leaders, Walsh captained the West Indies team 22 times.

*Courtney: Heart of the Lion* reads as a stirring tribute, but moves within the genre of hagiography rather than meaningful or critical biography. Ghosted by Derek Hodgson, it can't really decide whether it is autobiography or biography. It follows the routine formula of many sporting lives, concentrating on statistical information, dramatic incidents from particular matches – such as the Third Test at Barbados earlier this year when Brian Lara's phenomenal 153 not out and Courtney's match-

winning 0 not out won an astonishing test match against the Australians –
and flattering, if much deserved, descriptions of Walsh from team-mates
and opponents. But the great bowler deserves much better. There is little
narrative of his life and influences outside cricket, of the social forces which
have impinged upon the game in the Caribbean over the last two decades,
or of the political life of his home island and the whole Caribbean nation.

For Walsh has been an exemplary regional patriot and upholder of
Caribbean unity throughout his career in sport. He is the living and
symbolic human expression of Maurice Bishop's fervent cry, 'One
Caribbean!' As Michael Atherton emphasised, he 'always put regional
solidarity before island rivalry'. But he also fought hard for the rights of
professional cricketers across the region, struggling to lift their status and
provide Caribbean cricket with a secure economic base. Hodgson quotes an
elderly Jamaican cricket-lover who was angered at the threatened 'strike' of
West Indies cricketers and the frantic negotiations of Heathrow before the
1998 tour of South Africa. 'The players should be grateful because, if it
wasn't for Test Cricket, they would be picking cane,' he observed acerbically.
But Walsh has never stood for such servility and the touching of a colonial-
style forelock. Even after his demeaning and ungracious dismissal by
Gloucestershire after 14 years as an overseas professional, he maintained his
dignity, protested and passed on his thanks and regards to the thousands in
the county who loved and respected him.

Will he surpass the wickets of Hadlee and Kapil Dev? Time and the pace
bowler's tirelessness will tell. But the joy and powerful grace he has brought
to cricket, the humour of his batting and his irrepressible bowling energy
have already made him an international legend in the game.

Simon Rae:

# W.G. Grace

(*Morning Star*, 11 September 1999)

In the last paragraph of his monumental biography, *W.G. Grace*, Simon Rae
asserts that the image of Grace, 'a man with a beard, his bat poised
imperiously awaiting the next ball, will endure for as long as cricket is
played'. This most famous cricketer of all, he adds, has an unchallengeable
'place in the English consciousness'. For over a century, cricket has been

stuck within the confines of the image that was given to it by Grace and his era and it still struggles to be released from it.

For the boys and increasing numbers of girls who play in the streets, tarmac playgrounds and waste patches of their urban lives in northern and midland cities of England have a different cricketing ancestry. It is much more rooted in the Punjab or the Caribbean – closer to the Indus or the Demerara than the Thames or the Avon. Young white cricketers also owe much more to the brilliance and professional commitment of the journeymen players of the 'Golden Age' that followed, than to the priggish shamateurism that characterised Grace. None of which is to deny a great cricketer recognition.

But Grace 'detested radicals in politics' only a degree or so less than those umpires who had the temerity to give him out. He was also a diehard imperialist who saw cricket as having the power of agency to 'knit together the various sections of the British Empire and to advance the cause of civilisation'. Born in 1848 – a year of revolutions – he died in 1915 as the Zeppelins threatened his south London home. Yet, as Rae emphasised, he was a Gloucestershire family man, the head of a cricketing dynasty. His summers were spent playing and his winters were spent as a GP and West Country doctor attending his patients or dealing with the consequences of the frequent industrial accidents at local collieries.

How good was he? If you look at his achievements with both bat and ball, they are startling and Rae's book shows us this with clarity and eloquence. But how would he have coped against the fast bowling that was to follow him – the Larwoods, Lindwalls, Halls, Marshalls, Ambroses, Donalds or Shoaibs? In one of the finest passages of cricket narrative that I have read, Rae gives us the strongest of clues. A few days off his 50th birthday in 1898, Gloucestershire played Essex at Leyton and Grace's antagonist was the fastest bowler in the land – possibly, at that point in time, the fastest ever – Charles Kortright. Grace scored 126. Then fifty years on, Kortright told John Arlott: 'The Old Man made me look as simple as dirt. He wasn't attempting to hit the ball with the bat outside the off-stump, but he was punching it – punching it with his thick felt gloves'.

Of course, Grace played more than his fair share of suspect first-class games – Smokers against Non-smokers, Married against the Single, Over-30s and Under-30s, etc., etc., but his prestige as a cricketer was unchallenged – his rock-like defence and uncanny accuracy and placement of his shots, his phenomenal line and length as a bowler.

And all the time too, while enjoying the privileges of a 'gentleman' amateur, he made a prosperous living from the game – often subjecting the mere 'players' to the indignities of second-class travel or lousy hotel accommodation on the tours of Australia that he organised or captained.

Rae's biography is a tremendous book. It is a book to read, reflect upon and apply to sport and its superstars of our own era. What will be revealed of our world in the books that will be written about them a century hence?

Pete Davies:
# Mad Dogs and Englishwomen
(*Morning Star,* 13 July 1998)

On the reverse side of the entrance ticket to the final of the Women's Cricket World Cup Final at Eden Gardens cricket ground in Calcutta in December 1997, these words from the Indian sage Swami Vivekanandi, were printed:

*'There is no chance for the welfare of the world unless the condition of woman is improved. It is not possible for a bird to fly only on one wing.'*

Wise words and not immediately associated with a book about cricket. But such is the achievement of Pete Davies in his *Mad Dogs and Englishwomen* and even more of the 14 vibrant and skilful women that his book describes. The traditional 'men's game' of cricket is transformed to become an unlikely vehicle of the brain and body power of women players.

The cricket tour book holds a particular place within the literature of cricket. As a boy, I remember reading dozens of formulaically written and hurriedly published accounts of winter cricket tours rushed out at the beginning of the new season. With titles like *No Ashes For England, Caribbean Crusade* or *South African Journey,* they chronicled every match, often with a tedious exoticism or detachment from the actual, living experience of the people of the countries being toured. Indians, black South Africans, ordinary Australians, Trinidadians, Jamaicans, Barbadians or New Zealanders were made invisible. Writers like EW Swanton of the *Daily*

*Telegraph* or EM Wellings of the *Evening News* stiffly described the cricketers as bloodless and cardboard from their hotel rooms, golf courses or rarefied press boxes.

In Davies's book, India is the protagonist and its people have an equal coverage alongside the sportswomen. Like Mike Marqusee's vital and life-bursting story of the 1996 World Cup in India, Pakistan and Sri Lanka, entitled *War Minus the Shooting*, Davies's account transforms the model and genre of the cricket tour too. He describes scenes not to be found in previous 'cricket' books.

There is the boy who approaches his car window at a stop light, 'his left cheek was swollen out in some deformity, his face was a pleading rictus and his hand was a begrimed little bird fluttering at my arm, fingers like twigs.' There is the occasional step backwards into the tabloid caricature of the 'ramshackle' sun-drenched Third World, but the dominant theme of his description is to express not only the extremes of wealth generated by an India globalised and bayoneted by modern imperialism but also the hospitality, ingenuity, wit and warmth of its cricket-loving people – in particular its women.

As for the English cricket women, they are characterised strongly and individually by an admiring author. All amateurs, from PE teachers to travel agents, bank workers and the daughters of Midlands miners, they are nonplussed by the contrasts of India. Yorkshire woman Kathryn Long muses: 'It's an eye-opener, isn't it? ... To see a leper – you think it's something you'd only hear in a bible story.' Their tour – which is non-stop, frenetic and without any of the luxuries or sanitising experienced by elite professional sportsmen on the privileged circuit – ended in the semi-final against a formidable New Zealand team.

These women's ambitions and wishes were to be appreciated as serious cricketers with particular talents and not to be constantly compared to men. Their motivations exemplified sports people the world over and their story seen through the eyes and respect of Pete Davies makes fascinating reading. For, as their chronicler emphasised, they 'tackled an itinerary that the men would have turned down flat – tackled it for the simple reason that they all just wanted very badly to play cricket for their country. And that's why writing about people who play for love instead of money will always be more fun.'

Clyde Walcott with Brian Scovell:
# Sixty Years on the Back Foot
(*Morning Star*, 5 June 2000)

Who remembers the black cricketing whirlwind of the *Three Ws*? Frank Worrell – all grace and elegance and power at the crease, more-than-useful swing bowler and the first established black captain of the West Indies whose name is synonymous with Caribbean genius and unity. Everton Weekes, the relentlessly dominating batsman with shots all around the wicket who had a Test average of nearly 60 and who scored 4,500 runs in only 48 Test matches – few men have ever hit a cricket ball harder and with more consistency. And the third one, and author of *Sixty Years on the Back Foot*, Clyde Walcott. He was a big, big man and a huge, muscled batsman – a puller, cutter and driver who, on his many days, was merciless to bowlers and who also kept a sharp wicket, and could bowl medium pacers which were capable of shooting out the best batsmen.

All three of them were part of the same cricketing generation, all born within a mile of the Kensington Oval Test match ground in Barbados and all brought into the world of bat, ball, stumps and struggle by the same community midwife between 1924 and 1926. Has there ever been such an astonishing proximity of diverse talent spawned within such a small and singular sporting nursery as within those few rural roads in Barbados? And, as Walcott emphasises, they were always close friends and cricket comrades, never rivals. His story moves from his one small island to becoming not only one of the world's greatest batsman – in 1955 against Australia, for example, he scored 827 runs in five Tests, including five centuries – but also the first black chairman of the International Cricket Council and a roving ambassador for the future of the sport.

In 1992, while on a mission in South Africa, he visited the township of Alexandria near Johannesburg, 'occupying a speck of land totalling just one square mile' with 250,000 black people living there. Walcott, the Caribbean man, marvels and muses about his own home. 'Barbados has roughly 260,000 people living in 166 square miles and we say that it is overcrowded.'

Not surprisingly, the most fascinating parts of Walcott's story are the chapters about his halcyon playing days and his partnership with the other Ws. During the Lord's Test victory of 1950, Walcott scored 168 not out, a fearless innings which, together with the bowling feats of the prodigious young Trinidadian spinners Sonny Ramadhin and Alf Valentine, won the match for the West Indies. He became the bane of the English captain, Norman Yardley, and Lord Beginner, the calypsonian, celebrated and lionised him in his *Victory Test Match*:

> *Yardley wasn't broken-hearted*
> *When the second innings started.*
> *Jenkins was on the target*
> *Getting the first five into his basket*
> *Then Gomez broke them down*
> *While Walcott licked them around,*
> *He was not out for one sixty eight*
> *Leaving Yardley to contemplate.*

As he says, 'it was the first time that we had succeeded at cricket's headquarters and it was a symbolic moment in our lives and in the lives of our countrymen.'

Yet, the heart of his story is so often in its modesty, his appreciation of those with and against whom he played. He tells of his admiration of the furious fast bowling of Australian Ray Lindwall and the canny off-spin of Yorkshireman Jim Laker, who took his wicket 11 times in Tests. And he writes of his continuous evocations of Weekes and Worrell, the other triplets of brilliance. 'Whereas I specialised in powering the ball past fielders, Frank would glide it through them with perfect timing and style.'

Who could forget them, those of us privileged to remember their days in front of the wicket – emblems of a Caribbean glory.

Viv Richards:
## Sir Viv: The Definitive Autobiography
(*Morning Star*, 13 July 2000)

Perhaps every great sporting achiever deserves a second attempt at an autobiography and Viv Richard's *Sir Vivian* follows not too distantly after his first life-narration *Hitting Across the Line,* in 1991.

The titles themselves are indicators. By the year 2000, Richards is a cricketing knight and an OBE, as well as a celebrity guest and cricket coach of Brunei, working for the richest family in the world and living in, as he reflects, 'the height of luxury.' Yet none of this has eroded Richards's fire as Caribbean cricketer and critic – both are still central to this new testimony of life and sport. 'It is important to create intensity,' he declares – and no cricketer ever forged more than Viv Richards. His defiant stride to wicket, the whirling of the bat, the colours of Africa on his wrist, the maroon West Indies cap, which displaced the helmet all through his career – even against Thomson and Lillee at their most ferocious – such a prospect of black determination and audacity would overwhelm the tone and ambience of an entire match.

Richards's story is, above all, one of pride in being Caribbean – it is as if his communal commitments, primarily arise from his Antiguan reality. As a West Indian cricketer, his regional consciousness and love for all his contributing islands became the passion behind his batting genius. Like Bishop, Rodney, Marley or other West Indian iconic figures of his generation and before, such as CLR James, his cry was "One Caribbean."

Cricket is a binding, cultural force – as he observes in his book, 'islands so diverse and widespread, it is the one thing that brings everyone together as a nation.' And when cricket is down in the region, he recognises it as a symbol of the Caribbean's humanity racked by foreign economic interference and domestic 'buddyism' and elitism. As he walks around, he sees 'our people no longer holding their heads up high, it is as if they are tiptoeing in their own country because of the low level of confidence and self-esteem.'

When Richards confesses: 'I wore pride on my sleeve for everyone to see,' we remember the African wristband and contempt for the rands of apartheid. The South Africans prized a futile hope of him breaking the sporting boycott above all others, offering him £500,000 to play on an apartheid pitch. Of course, he refused, to his eternal credit. He writes that 'the money was not a consideration. I was simply not interested in such a thing. I knew of the sufferings going on in South Africa and was insulted when it was suggested to me that, if I went, I would be called an honorary white. That is as low as you can get in selling your soul.' They are words which, recalling the events that they chronicle, inspire the great human essence of sport.

*Sir Viv* is written with verve and the subject's competitive and obdurate cricketing personality comes compellingly through. His uproarious and wild years with Ian Botham playing in Somerset and setting Taunton alight, his marvellous exploits in Clive Lloyd's incredible team, his tribute to his lost comrade-in-arms, Barbadian Malcolm Marshall, his intervals in Glamorgan and Rishton in the Lancashire League – all take life and moment from his writing.

There is an observation which seems to worry and torment him, even as he writes it. 'I have always looked upon myself as being a rebel and now, suddenly, it seems that I am part of the Establishment,' Richards says. I doubt it and anyone else who has been inspired by his life and brilliance would probably doubt it too.

Ted Corbett:
# The Great Cricket Betting Scandal
(*Morning Star*, 25 July 2000)

No, this is not a rushed-out account of the Hansie Cronje saga or a narrative on the Mark Waugh/Shane Warne Australian gambling shenanigans. In fact, *The Great Cricketing Betting Scandal* is historical fiction, telling of imperial skulduggery, with cricket as its conduit, on a pioneering tour of India made by an MCC team in 1906.

Yet the story whips back to the Edwardian past from the future. In the year 2007, John Goode, 'the first black man to captain England' – what about Essex man Nasser Hussain, then? – is given, along with his appointment, a series of briefings and commissions by officers and ministers of state. In fact, cricket itself, Corbett is implying, was, in its 'golden-age' heyday, in reality an activity of state and its commanding authority, the MCC, which was then virtually a state institution in itself, was an instrument of empire.

Goode is taken into and along the 'hide-aways, underground passages and quiet, not to say secret rooms' below the Lord's pavilion and introduced to some shadowy figures who impress upon him that to be captain of England is to be more than a cricketer – he must also be a spy, diplomat, economic fixer and gubernatorial representative. To illustrate this, he is given a cautionary tale – a manuscript of a journal of the 1906 tour of India written by the captain of the time, one Bernard Collinson. The journal details the special imperial tasks given to Collinson in his day and the pressure mounted upon him to ensure that he accomplished them.

As he describes his appointment, Collinson is revealed as something of a closet socialist – the grammar school-educated son of an ex-army officer and a Japanese mother, whose short tenure as a player for Yorkshire was undermined by the county club's racist attitude toward his mother – a piercing comment on the deep roots of Yorkshire racism. So he joined Surrey and eventually graduated to captain England against the Indians, who, he is told by no less a figure than ex-Viceroy Lord Curzon, 'are as tricky as any race on earth.'

Collinson's adventures on the tour are told with wit, candour and humour through Corbett's pacy and sharp narrative style. Surrounded and besieged by Westminster bureaucrats and espionage experts and seduced by women involved in security and gambling scams on two continents, the fortunate and unfortunate Collinson is characterised as an amalgam of Tom Brown, James Bond and Ian Botham. At the same time, Corbett's ironical style sends-up the imperial connections of cricket past, while running an implied commentary on the big-time profiteering betting syndicates and corrupted officials and infrastructures of cricket present. As one of his own team-mates, who is up to his neck in gambling rackets, declares in words which would find empathy with Hansie, 'it is not a crime to bet against one's own team, however damnable that might seem.'

Corbett brings together fictional characters with past cricketing icons, such as Jack Hobbs and Wilfred Rhodes, to create a sporting yarn which turns out to be wholly entertaining, sharp with historical insight and more than a little prophetic.

Leo McKinstrey:
## Boycs: The True Story
(*Morning Star*, 29 June 2000)

Despite the familiar affability of its title and its leasehold from the county cricket changing rooms, *Boycs* is less a biography than a portrait of the contradictions of a Janus-like batsman – someone who is probably more loved and more loathed than any other player in the entire professional game and its hinterland.

The arresting photograph on the cover does not show Geoff Boycott in his days of batting glory, scoring his hundredth century or holding up an England innings while all fall around him. Instead, the Yorkshireman is dressed in smart jacket and tie, wearing his Panama hat and the lopsided smile. You can almost hear the dialect which is so well-known by the entire cricket world, as John Arlott's Hampshire tones were known, imitated and caricatured from Barbados to Brisbane, from Calcutta and Lahore to Lords.

Boycott's origins were in Fitzwilliam, a mining village near Wakefield, where he lived with his mother in a terraced house with an outside toilet until he was in his mid-twenties. His father was a pit roadlayer who was severely injured in 1950 by a coal tub as he was mending the track by the coal-face. He was an 11-plus failure who became one of cricket's wealthiest men – as player, pundit and television commentator, the sport's most successful and high profile world rover.

McKinstrey writes of Boycott being 'baffled by his own contradictions' and such point and counterpoint become the theme of his book. 'Most people who played with him thought the guy was a pillock, never gave a damn about anyone else,' declares a contemporary batsman and Boycott's room-mate on tour, Frank Hayes. 'He was dedicated to the exclusion of everyone else,' says Tony Lewis, who captained him. Yet others speak of him as generous and warm-hearted, a genuine 'people's player'.

His reputation shattered by accusations of misogyny and violence to women, McKinstrey quotes many examples of Boycott's verbal aggression and chauvinism, but also many compliments from women who know him well. As for his 'Yorkshireness,' bowler John Lever attests that 'he could be rude and hide behind his Yorkshire bluntness as an excuse'. Yet, at Headingley in 1977, when he scored his century of centuries in a Test match against the Australians, thousands of Yorkshiremen and women saluted him as their favourite son.

But the reader is left with this summation from McKinstrey's paradoxical portrait. Despite Boycott's profound and all-embracing knowledge of the game, his frequent prescience as critic and commentator and his prodigious achievements as an opening batsman for twenty years against some of the mightiest fast bowlers of his generation, he remains cricket's archetypal Thatcherite. As Thatcher – whom Boycott, even with his pit lineage, steadfastly admires – believed that there was no community, no society excepting that which promotes and profits the individual, the same may apply to Boycott. There is no team, only the self as player, no total score, only I, the batsman's single innings.

His way of playing was not for the benefit of cricket and its essential collective people's culture in Yorkshire villages or other struggling places across the world, from Fitzwilliam and its unemployed youth to those in Soweto too. As for all Thatcher's disciples, so for Boycott. It was money - £50,000 converted from South African rands in 1982 for organising a 'rebel' tour as the apartheid machine of racism and death was at its most intense and forbidding. And it was a time when other great cricketers of his era – notably, Botham and Richards, Marshall and Gower – refused Boycott's blandishments and the persuasive sponsorship of Holiday Inn Incorporated of the US. Boycs – not so much an enigma as an entrepreneur of cricket. And also a sad distortion of such guts and determination in front of the wicket for all those years.

Pat Symes:

# Maco: The Malcolm Marshall Story

(*Morning Star*, 1 September 2000)

The world of cricket has found it very difficult to believe that Malcolm Marshall is dead. Since November 1999, memories of the Barbadian fast bowler – who took 376 Test wickets, mostly through the 1980s – have been as momentous as any in the game.

*Maco* describes his last desperate struggle against cancer of the colon and the grief at his death. It covers the assemblage of world cricketers at his funeral at St Bartholomew's Church close to his island's international airport where echoes of his own airspeed were all around as the tributes were paid to him. They frame a reprinting of his cricketing autobiography with the profoundly fitting title *Marshall Arts*. Hampshire-born cricket journalist Pat Symes collaborated on that first book and has also compiled *Maco*, adding a reflective tailpiece to every chapter.

Marshall's cricketing genius is closest to two other brilliant fast bowlers, one English and the other Australian. Like Harold Larwood and Ray Lindwall, who were icons of their own eras, Marshall was lightning-quick, yet was not a tall man and did not gain unusual bounce through height. His deliveries were even more menacing because of their lower trajectory and unerring accuracy. His superb bowling rhythm and letting loose of the ball through meteoric arm movement combined with an exceptional control and outstanding bowling intelligence.

When CLR James wrote about the 'great West Indian brains' of the best Caribbean cricketers, he could have been predicting the prescience and analytical mind of Marshall. He enjoined this with unflagging preparation and planning – ensuring that he studied batsmen whom he was due to play against through close observation and, latterly as they became available, through film and video. He was the nonpareil of the modern, technical cricketer, but could only be so because of his outstanding physical discipline and natural skill which was enhanced by brilliant technique. Symes's commentary tells stories of Maco's ability to bowl in-swing and away-swing ball-by-ball to order. He could put the ball anywhere that he chose at a ferocious speed and deliver wicket-taking balls according to the carefully diagnosed weakness of the batsman – whether playing for West Indies, Hampshire or Barbados.

The autobiographical trunk of the book is Marshall's modest but revealing story of his passage from an unpromising youth, when he found himself 'unemployed and with no realistic chance of getting any work.' Thus cricket came to him like a saviour. He writes very openly and honestly about his successes – like his virtual single-handed victory as the injured 'one-armed bandit' over England at the 1984 Headingley Test. But he also lists his failures and driving forces like the humiliation he felt after his first, unfair test match dismissal by the Indian Dilip Vengsarkar. He describes too the terrible temptations and lures dangled in front of him by the apartheid South African cricket authorities who offered him a cool $1 million to tour in 1983, but who got an even cooler rejection.

One of the truly great bowlers was Malcolm Marshall. Whether you saw him in the lucid light of the Caribbean or under the grey clouds of a Bournemouth late afternoon, you were watching a master of cricketing culture and a luminous Caribbean man to his very bones.

David Thurlow:
# Ken Farnes: Diary of an Essex Master
(*Morning Star,* 18 July 2000)

Every sport has its own devotees and dedicated scholars, who, through their meticulous research and painstaking investigation, open up the lives and times of its players and achievers. In his *Ken Farnes: Diary of an Essex Master*, David Thurlow uncovers both a man and a cricketing era.

The man is Kenneth Farnes, who was killed in October 1941 during a night-time flight while practising for bombing raids over Germany. His gravestone reads: 'He died as he lived, playing the game.' A common enough epitaph for the life of a pre-war cricketer, but Farnes was uncommon enough. Faster than any other bowler of the immediate post-Larwood generation, in its obituary, *The Times* crystallised his enigmatic on-pitch personality. 'He was, perhaps, a bowler of moods, either destructively hostile or complacently amicable, but, in his full fighting feathers, he was a danger to any batsman in the world.'

From a cricketing family in the Essex suburbs, I grew up with Farnes's memory as a boyhood icon. My father had opened the bowling with this shy six-and-a-half footer in his days as a local club cricketer and he remembered Farnes's phenomenal bounce and speed of pitch – a white Joel Garner or Curtly Ambrose of his day. And a Romford rebel too. Despite his childhood memories and poetic descriptions of the 'green' and local parks where he learned his cricket, the blue suburban skies of comfort and contentment, he became a reluctant and resentful commuter to work in a London bank, crushed into the carriages from Gidea Park to Liverpool Street stations with thousands of other greyly besuited City office workers. 'I conceived a bitter hatred of a London that was a virtual prison for me,' he wrote and, during the summer of 1930, he went to watch the Australians play Essex at Leyton instead of going to work and never went back to his office.

Instead he became a teacher and, during his school holidays, an amateur for Essex and England in the years before the outbreak of war. He toured the Caribbean, Australia and South Africa after taking 10 wickets in his first match against Bradman and the Australians in 1934.

A reserved and cultured man, he painted, read broadly and wrote a modest autobiography, *Tours and Tests*. In it he described the bruised colouration of an Essex team-mate's thighs the morning after facing Larwood at his fastest. 'It would have made Turner sigh, for no sunset of his could have equalled the vividness of pigment and such a range of hues.'

While on tour in South Africa during the winter of 1938-39, Farnes wrote a fascinating journal of an attempt to get close to 'realising my 'self'.' Having met a group of east London children before his outward voyage, whose poverty 'seemed a horrible reflection on the state of civilisation in education,' his reflections on the conditions of black workers at Kimberley's diamond mines provoked even greater shock. He wrote how they were imprisoned in the mine compound – 'one boy had been there for 13 years without going out.' It makes the reader wonder where the journey of Farnes's 'self' would have led had he survived the war.

Thurlow has written an important and deeply moving book about a neglected sportsman and the light and darkness of his times. He reminds us of one particular statistic from a cricket scorebook which reads like an elegy of its era. In the fifth Test at Melbourne in 1937, the Australian batsman Ross Gregory was caught by the Yorkshire spinner Hedley Verity off the bowling of Farnes for 80. Thus, the scorebook read: *RG Gregory c Verity b Farnes 80*. All three, two of them airmen and Verity an infantry officer during the 1943 invasion of Sicily, were to perish in the war against fascism.

Sport and life – never to be separated!

# 11.

# PITCH OF LIFE
## Re-reading C.L.R. James' Beyond a Boundary

AT THE HEADINGLEY TEST MATCH during the frigid English June of 1991, I was watching the progress of the West Indies first innings. It was late afternoon, and by that time much drinking had been done around the ground. It was a cold, cold Saturday which had been warmed by two inspirational pieces of cricket from the young Ramprakash, a newcomer to the England team whose family roots were planted first in India, then on the coastal lowlands of Guyana and the streets of London. He had launched himself sideways to take one brilliant catch to dismiss Simmons, then minutes after thrown down the stumps from mid-wicket after a lightning pick-up to create another wicket from nowhere. Those two electric acts had sparked the cutting atmosphere of the iciest cricket-watching day that I can ever remember.

Until about 4.30 in the afternoon – for then it was the time of Viv Richards. As he strode out to the wicket with his implacable gait, unhelmeted and unperturbed by climate, crowd, match conditions or apparently anything else around him, a lone and dreadlocked West Indies supporter standing near the players' steps let out a loud cheer and Caribbean words of brotherhood and encouragement. The bond and magnetism of his cry was urgent and powerful. A group of white spectators standing near him, carrying their lager cans, slurring their words and grimacing their aggression, turned on him and Richards too with curses, racist insults and crude, provocative gestures. He stood his ground as Viv always did, giving back everything piled upon him until other spectators intervened and warned off the insulters.

Now Headingley is certainly not the most friendly or hospitable grounds in England for black cricketers and their supporters. Yorkshire cricket, its administrators and followers have often been as cold as this June Saturday in receiving and recognising the talents of black British cricketers. The 'no foreigners' approach to Yorkshire cricket and its century-long refusal to allow anyone not born in Yorkshire to play for the county before it opened its doors for prestige overseas players like Sachin Tendulkar and Richie Richardson, has meant that still not one single cricketer from the squads of excellent black cricketers playing every weekend in the leagues and inner cities of Yorkshire had been selected. Many of these, disrespected, excluded and ignored, have gone to form their own teams and leagues to play against each other, and have thus been forced into a Jim Crow cricket arrangement in the cities and old mill towns of northern England.

So when these drunken Headingley spectators spat out their invective at Viv Richards and his countryman they were the worst of the cricket world insulting and trying to humiliate the best. The dreadlocked watcher was brave and full of resistance and had, no doubt, had to confront similar menaces before on the streets of Leeds or other places in England. Viv, too, of course, was no stranger to such hostility, and more than once in his career took on the gibes of taunting spectators, British journalists and their press campaigns, and the violence of Australian attitudes during the 1975 tour.[1] As he wrote in *Hitting Across the Line*[2]: 'We came up against extreme savagery in that series, what many people would call extreme racism. Now what is a West Indian bouncer compared to that?'. There is a perennial image of Viv Richards in my head, and it is of him walking to the wicket. The pride, the matchless inner confidence that shines out, the assuredness of movement, the purple cap as if an integral part of the scalp. Here were a whole proud people going out to bat and to com-bat, a ray of Caribbean nationhood and the proud individual citizen of that nation, from a small island yet knowing no smallness, only power and readiness. That is why that lone, proudly-locked black man could resist and feel no sense of impending defeat from a group of cowardly and pathetic racists. There was a rock-like compatriot before him, striding towards the struggle of his people's cricket – and no bitter or envious postcolonial word-lash or threat was going to turn him around. In his autobiography Richards wrote of the 'deep, deep love' that binds cricketers and cricket-lovers from the Caribbean, a love and solidarity which beamed out from his own cricket directly from 'that self-belief about finding that inner strength, that determination…in the face of all manner of adversity and negative influence.'[3] Who was ever going to make Viv Richards or his Headingley brother 'grovel'? He was a great innovator of Caribbean cricket insurgency, but he also inherited the insights and understanding of pioneering forbears like Learie Constantine of Trinidad who, like him, knew of the aggression which surrounded the cricket world in which he played, with its 'failing intelligence…clinging to its wars and inequalities, its racial barriers and shibboleths.'[4]

## Viv's Example

I believe that this incident at Headingley crystallises the effect of Viv Richards on his region's cricket, but also on his people. There is a parallel too with the deeds and words of Maurice Bishop. Viv was a symbol for the Grenada Revolution and those who led it on their small, struggling island. They saw him, as C.L.R. James would have expressed it, 'as their man', but also the whole Caribbean's man, their living emblem and inspiration too: the anti-imperial cricketer, the free West Indian of the crease. As Bishop had a dream of 'One Caribbean!', of a world where imperialism would be 'hit for six', so Richards too manifested the region's essential unity. 'Our pride in the West Indies binds us all together. If only we could work together. Perhaps sport should be the model for all life.' And as Bishop's words and Grenada's achievement sought to repel the new imperialism, the Reaganism of the north to 'Leave Grenada alone! Leave the Caribbean people alone! Leave the Revo alone!'[5], so Richards declares in *Hitting Across the Line*: 'I want to warn people to stop their racism. I want them to leave the West Indies cricket alone!'[6] For there has never been a cricketer so proud and combative as Viv Richards. Before him Constantine, Weekes, Walcott, Gilchrist, Hall, Griffith and Lloyd had brought a concentrated power, Headley, Worrell, Sobers and Gibbs a certain grace, fluency and phenomenal talent, and Ramadhin, Valentine, Collie Smith and Kanhai a unique ingenuity and creative genius. But Richards brought all these with a sense of assertive dignity, self-confidence and outright challenge that made the racists boil and his own people come out with all their strength and defiance of oppression. He was a product of the Caribbean cricketing achievement that came before, but provoked its emulation in others through the Caribbean and across the diaspora. And by looking in contempt upon the rand and turning his back on those who sought to use cricket to buy time for Apartheid, he inspired others, black and white, to do the same. The greatest prize for its upholders, along with Richards himself, was Ian Botham. But Botham could not look into his friend's eye if he had gone to South Africa, so thus he stayed away. As the contemporary of Marley, of Bishop, of Walter Rodney, of Caribbean women like Jacqueline Creft or Merle Hodge – as well as Holding, Marshall, Roberts, Garner and Greenidge, he played for a generation of courage and creation too, across the many currents and depths of culture through the Caribbean.

It did not occur to me on that Headingley Saturday, that it would be Richards' countryman and successor to the captaincy, Richie Richardson, truly the metaphorical son of the father, who would do much to help break down the racism in Yorkshire cricket. For that is what he did when he became the county's second overseas player during the 1994 season. He is absolutely his own man and his own brilliant cricketer, but perhaps Richards' huge and empowering courage also moved him. So our young black cricketers here at school, rushing to their lunch hour practices and squeezing in some five-a-side between the end of the afternoon school and the beginning of mosque, chalking up stumps anywhere there is street space or a brick wall and listening closely to the cricketing experience of their Jamaican coach – perhaps they too, in the heart of a Yorkshire inner city, owe a debt of emulation to Viv Richards. As we all do.

In his vibrant and beautifully presented coaching manual, *Cricket Masterclass* – a gift of a cricketing experience to any young enthusiast, Richards declares: 'Work at the basics but never be afraid to do something different. My fundamental wish for every cricketer is to keep his panache while observing the basic principles.'[7] Sound rules for life itself, and a grounding for Caribbean cricket also voiced by Constantine. 'Try to contribute something new,' he advised, 'and carry the spirit of your cricket into your life.'[8] It is that very sense of difference, a different courage to challenge and overcome domination, racial arrogance and injustice, that we take from Viv Richards into our lives with the memories of the wristband of African colours swinging with the arm-whirls of the bat and uncompromising step, forward ever, towards the contest in the middle.

That was Viv Richards at his cricket and for millions his example can never fade.

Such words of praise for Viv Richards could never have come to me without the agency of C.L.R. James and his book of sport and book of life, *Beyond a Boundary.*[9] In this book James reaches three monumental purposes. First he identifies sport, one particular sport – cricket - as a vehicle of popular struggle, in his instance, of anti-imperialism, anti-racism and as an enemy of colonialism. He expresses cricket aesthetically, seeing the sport as a discourse of beauty and human culture. And finally and most importantly, he sees cricket as not simply a metaphor of life but as life itself, a way of approaching the challenges of being and living in the world: 'How do men live?' he asks – or more exactly 'what do men live by?' Of course James was a man, largely speaking to other men, who played and loved a particular sport which bespoke a particular culture in a specific age. In these senses *Beyond a Boundary* may be criticised as limited, even ephemeral. Yet in its ability to connect a pursuit of leisure to the mainsprings of human life's essential progress, it is a book which has no equal.

James wrote of the Trinidadian batsman, Wilton St. Hill, that 'as soon as he started to stride to the wicket everyone stopped what he was doing and paid attention.'[10] Viv Richards had the same effect on spectators that day at Headingley. For Caribbean watchers he was their hero, their symbol of dynamic energy and progress. For white racist spectators he personified success, fearlessness, power and therefore danger. A few weeks ago I heard Gary Sobers, perhaps the greatest, the most versatile and complete of Caribbean cricketers, talk in Sheffield. After his presentation I asked him about his thoughts on Roy Gilchrist, the Jamaican fast bowler who I had seen bowl against Essex at Ilford in 1957. I had never, and I think, have since never, seen bowling so fast and fierce. In his first over to the Essex opening batsman, the cavalier 'dasher' Dickie Dodds, he bowled a ball that hurtled over the batsman and wicket-keeper (who was Clyde Walcott, not a small man) and hit the sightscreen on the first bounce. I hardly saw it before I heard the crash and saw the umpire signal four vertical wides. 'Ah Gilchrist!' said Sobers, 'now he was the most *dangerous* cricketer I ever played with.' Perhaps that was why he couldn't last, why the black and uncompromising Gilchrist was so prematurely dismissed and rejected from the international game for his hostility to the last West Indian light-skinned captain, Gerry Alexander, - and it was only the fact that Richards, with all his similar 'danger', arrived into cricket two generations later, that he could survive, prosper and conquer so formidably.

As he tells us in *Beyond a Boundary*, James took up the case of Gilchrist as he was later to mobilise and lead the campaign for the West Indies captaincy to be given to the obvious and outstanding candidate – the black man Frank Worrell. It was, as he writes, a part of his commission to 'lay racialism flat and keep stamping on it whenever it raises its head.'[11] It is such commitment and achievement through writing, organising and leading cricketing struggles against racism that has made *Beyond the Boundary* a classic manual and inspiration for standing up to all forms of Jim Crow and prejudice in cricket, in small ways as in large. The book is a constant source of challenge for those cricketers and cricket lovers involved, for example, in the campaigning in Britain of 'Hit Racism for Six',[12] the only existing organisation nationally established for coordinating anti-racist activities within the sport. In its work to expose the ugly attitudes within powerful interests at the heart of cricket – for example in the established cricket journalism of *Wisden's Cricket Monthly* and the vicious article by Robert Henderson attacking black English cricketers, the example of James' own combative journalism and message in *Beyond a Boundary* played a major influence. The campaign resulted in black county and international players like Devon Malcolm and Philip de Freitas winning their High Court case against the article and receiving substantial compensation (a proportion of which Malcolm donated to Sheffield's Devon Malcolm Cricket Centre, established to bring coaching and other resources to young inner city cricket enthusiasts). Similarly, those insights of James about the behaviour of cricket crowds – the responses to cricketers of 'the people who watch them', those too who crowd into Lord's, Trent Bridge and Old Trafford who 'bring with them the whole past history and future hopes' of their people. They also bring, as I discovered in their reactions to Viv Richards and his Rastafarian comrade in 1991 at Headingley, all their prejudices and the detritus and residue of their imperial minds, if they are Englishmen.

## Racism on the Western Terrace

In August 1995 I found myself in the centre of another crowd-scene at Headingley, this time sitting on the Western Terrace during the second test match against Pakistan, and listening to the violent racist language and physical aggression of white sections of the crowd against Pakistani players on the pitch, and groups of Asian spectators who were part of the crowd. Inhuman, murderous shouts were interspersed with violent drunken outbreaks of jostling and outright physical challenge. The campaigning around exposing and opposing the outrage of this Headingley behaviour was led by 'Hit Racism for Six', and included a strongly featured article in the *Observer*[13] written by myself, very much moved by the conscious spirit of James' cricketing journalism in Trinidad in the fifties.

*As the slow train between Sheffield and Leeds made its way through the blighted and jobless towns of the Dearne Valley – Bolton upon Dearne, Thurscoe, Fitzwilliam, there came the first ominous comment. A group of young men going to Headingley for the Saturday of the test match against Pakistan were reading the ground regulations printed on their ticket supplements: 'Racial abuse is strictly forbidden' one of them quoted. 'Ah, until teatime any road!' added his mate.*

*Inside the ground, on the Western Terrace, I waited with my 11 year old son and his Pakistani friend for the day's play to begin. Rain had held it up for an hour. There was more space then usual; every third row of seating had been removed for better crowd control following disturbances during last year's test match. Majority support was white – with many spectators wearing football shirts. But a strong Asian contingent sat in clusters.*

*A superabundance of stewards from a private security firm, dressed in luminous red and yellow jackets with 'Crowd control, crowd safety' printed on their backs, patrolled the terraces. For a reason no one could fathom, they blocked the main path through the bottom of the rows of seats, sending spectators to walk along the congested and narrow spacing between tight rows of seated England and Pakistan supporters. They were officious and uncompromising, and got up the nose of almost everyone there – soon becoming the butts of humour and abuse.*

*At lunchtime the atmosphere was friendly and inter-active: someone had brought a bunch of large beach balls, which were punched and slapped around the terraces. It was good-humoured and brought the crowd together – until, one by one, the balls were captured by the stewards to a unity of booing from almost all spectators.*

*The drinking grew apace. A group of Yorkshire lads in front of me were stepping up the volume and with it abuse at passers by. They shredded up copies of the* Sun, *the* Star *and the property section of the* Yorkshire Post *and flung the small pieces in the air every time a section of the crowd attempted an abortive Mexican wave. A young man with long, slicked-down hair became their particular target: 'Drown the witch! Drown the witch!' they chanted every time he passed by. It was an anachronism, but a vile and menacing one at that, and seemed like another omen.*

*Just after tea, an elderly white man managed to defeat the cordon of stewards blocking the main route through the terrace. He was cheered by everybody, white and Asian. Then a youth in a Pakistan shirt tried the same tactic, failed and was held by three white stewards. Suddenly, in a second, scores of white spectators were on their feet, hurling abuse – now not at the stewards, but at the restrained Asian youth. A white youth, clearly out of his head with drink, came hurtling downwards from the top of the terrace, crashing into the held Asian youth, and punching him. Other Pakistan supporters came forward to protect their friend as a group of stewards and police descended from the upper terraces, grabbing three Asian youths including the challenger of the cordon, and pulled them back up the terrace.*

*In an instant it was as if a boil had been pricked and the pus of four centuries of Empire was pulsing out. White spectators behind the boys and me were screaming 'Stab the Pakis!' Abuse was coming from all directions. Spectators with a medley of football shirts from Middlesbrough to Newcastle to the Rangers were belching out insults. Beer was thrown over Pakistan supporters in the front rows. As a group of middle-aged Asians protested half way back up the terraces, they too were pounced upon and led away by stewards and police. White spectators around them chanted their support for the police: 'Take them out! Take them out! Take them out!'*

*This was not blind yobbery. It was the spillage of racism, incontrovertible and putrid. My son's friend sat through it all, apparently bemused, but with who knows what happening inside him. An Asian woman walked past with a small child: 'Let's have a look at yer chapatti, love,' shouted out a young man to my left, as a group of other Englishmen dressed as spoof Moslems screamed abuse and made feigned bows towards the Pakistani supporters in front of them. Racism and sexism were feeding off each other, while Alex Stewart reached his century and Waqar toiled without success from the football ground end.*

*A Pakistan supporter, dubbed 'Omar Sharif' by the spectators in front of me, made a harmonious gesture by going around groups of white supporters with a bowl of cooked chicken pieces. Some accepted them thanking him – others took them and thrust them back at him, hostilely and insultingly.*

*As for me, I had seen and heard enough, as I am sure my son and his friend had too, and we made our way up the chaotic and fuming terraces onto the perimeter path that runs along the rear.*

*I felt angry all the way home: there was the customary racist partiality of the police and private security firms, the failure of the senior England players sitting on their balcony one hundred yards away to come down and use their influence with the crowd – and the shameful behaviour of hundreds of young Englishmen.*

*The next day's papers criticised the 'yobbery' but there was very little about racism – only an oblique statement by Sir Lawrence Byford, the president of the Yorkshire County Cricket club. 'Use your own eyes!' he declared, when a journalist asked if the behaviour on the terraces was caused by 'racial undertones.'*
*'Undertones' is the most inept word to use. There were racist overtones, right over the length and breadth of the Western Terrace that Saturday*

*afternoon – loud, clear and squalid. And these were not the voices of organised fascists – although they would have been overjoyed at these events. More like the sounds of a grotesque carnival of Sun-readers, Murdoch-men, clones of tabloid chauvinism and racism, proud to be British, afraid to be human.*

*No other event has persuaded me so much of the imperative need not only for antiracist campaigns like 'Hit Racism for Six' to penetrate the heart of English cricket and its race and class complexes and prejudices, but the importance of reviving antiracist education among young people in schools, colleges and workplaces. Government and OFSTED give this low regard and little importance, and resources and priorities in schools have turned aside from its necessity over the last decade.*

*Headingley's Western Terrace shows why such work is essential: and why any future social equity and coherence in British cities depend upon it.*

In matters large and small, from great stadia to public parks and school playgrounds, in the dialectic between the personal and the political. For the protests of James also fired me to take up cricket-based protests in the intimacies of my own sporting and family life. When, while playing for my local club in the Sheffield League, an opposing player called my own six year old mixed-race son a 'bloody ethnic' when he accidentally stepped on one of his pads while I was in the field, I was determined to follow through his ignorance and racism to the heart of the league, which after some strong correspondence from officers of my own club, secured an acknowledgement and apology from the club concerned. I can say that without doubt with reference to my own life and I know the same is true for many others – that reading James has led directly to action and struggle for progress. Thus is the true work of words – words about a sport which at times may have been at the centre of our lives and affected much more on its margins.

## The Window

In August 1982 I interviewed James in his bedsitting room in Brixton, south London.[14] At that time, I had recently returned from a two-year period working as a teacher educator and English lecturer in Grenada for the People's Revolutionary Government. We did not discuss cricket. I wanted to ask James his views on language and power, particularly how he saw the tensions and alliances between the Caribbean vernacular and Standard English. Yet all the time we dealt with these questions, he kept his television on, with a very slight volume, at the foot of his bed as he lay along it. Frequently he would look up at it. For much of the interview the English left-hander David Gower was batting, and James nodded or exclaimed from time to time as he played a handsome stroke or the bowlers gained some life from the wicket or showed their own skills. It seemed to me, watching him and remembering the early evocative passages of *Beyond a Boundary*, that in his old age, James was connecting with that view of cricket from his boyhood bedroom, stretching towards the window sill to look out over the cricket field of Tunapuna, Trinidad. Now the window was this small, portable television screen, enabling him to watch over a world view of cricket and still shape his 'impressions of personality in society.' It was a long, long journey from the plebeian, snarling Matthew Bondman of his boyhood, now to the casual pose and batting elegance of the debonair Gower, but I remember how James described the transformation of the former when he took hold of a cricket bat: 'So crude and vulgar in every aspect of his life, with a bat in his hand he was all grace and style.'[15] For me, *Beyond a Boundary* was a book which itself became a window through which I could transform my own view of the world, and its expression through cricket. Thus James' work about this cultural activity that was so dear to my own early life, cut deeper into my mind than any theoretical work could ever manage.

All the time we discussed the implications of decolonising language, James continually referred back to his boyhood, his saturation in Standard English through his early reading of the Bible, Shakespeare and Thackeray. He spoke of one great colonial cultural institution while turning his head to keep vigil on another as it was played at the foot of his bed. He spoke of power through language – not only in the sense of the acculturated power of the coloniser's language, but how the new black and Caribbean writers – from Earl Lovelace, Linton Kwesi Johnson, Wole Soyinka, to popular singers like the calypsonian The Mighty Sparrow, were bringing a new energy, dynamism and power to the language of black literature and society.

His references to this new generation of writers and their bursting of language reminded me of his descriptions in *Beyond a Boundary* of the Trinidadian fast bowler, George John, and it took me back twenty years to my own days at school. Let me explain.

James describes George John as a powerful element of a 'generation of black men bowling fast'[16] that was 'more sure of itself' than those who came before. Although they were still under the control of white colonial cricket controllers and captains, they were gaining in their confidence – and sometimes suffering for their boldness. John, asserts James, never held back in making his 'cricketing anger' clear and explicit. He was the true forebear of formidable generations of cricketers who played with Sobers, under Lloyd and alongside Richards: 'Everything they were came into cricket with them.'[17] Their English equivalents were Trueman, Milburn or Lock. They gave all of themselves to the truth and sincerity of their art, so that their cricketing expression was wholly themselves. They wore no masks: they were authentic humans on the pitch of life.

James, having described John's particular cricket genius with great skill and a moving sense of personal remembrance, concludes his chapter by talking about the fast bowler's son, Errol. Now in 1963, when I was a Shakespeare-loving schoolboy hungry for the canon of English literature – from a cricket-worshipping lower middle-class home in the London suburbs, I encountered Errol John. As James tells us, he was an actor and a playwright, whose poignant play set in the barrack yards of Port of Spain, *Moon on a Rainbow Shawl*,[18] had won the *Observer* drama prize for 1957. He had appeared in Hollywood films and as the 1962-63 Old Vic season programme notes to *Othello*[19] and *The Merchant of Venice* tell us, he was a fellow of the Guggenheim Foundation of New York. Ironically, as English teacher in Bishop's High School, Tobago in 1968-9, I sought permission of my headteacher to produce *Moon on a Rainbow Shawl* as the yearly school play. It was told that I could not – the play had too much 'spicey' and 'local' language, 'low-life' characters and its form of strong social realism would not be considered appropriate by the parents. It was also the tradition, I was reminded, that the school every year produced extracts from Shakespeare's plays, and that tradition should continue. After much persuasion, I managed to convince the Head that we should write our own play on a local theme and perform it. We did so, putting together a play about the human consequences of the 1963 tragedy in Tobago of Hurricane Flora and winning the National Schools Arts Festival with it – but that is another story.[20] I was certainly forbidden to produce Errol John's play in his own land, and that of C.L.R. James too, for fear of embarrassment of language and reality, and for fear of cultural shame.

But back to 1963 and the Old Vic season. John played Othello, and also had the minor typecast and 'black' part of the Prince of Morocco in *The Merchant of Venice* ('dislike me not for my complexion…'). But a black man playing Othello was still an unusual enough event, despite the huge success in the part of the American Paul Robeson both before and after the war. Errol John, however, was a Caribbean man, a Trinidadian – like those calypsonians who arrived on the 'Empire Windrush' or celebrated the West Indian cricket victory over England at Lord's in 1950 with their burst of song and satirical lyrics. And although he was a trained classical actor, the Trinidadian foundation to his voice was still as strong as it was beautiful. I saw the production, looking down from the gallery over a three-quarters empty theatre, and was much moved by it, as I was to the vulnerable dignity given to the main character by Errol John, and to me – the unusually melodic and un-English intonation and cadences of his speech which contrasted with the hardness of sound of the Iago of the Australian Leo McKern. Yet when I read the reviews of the production and of John's performance I remember reacting with surprise and anger. Almost to a man (and they were all men) the reviewers condemned John for his speaking of Shakespeare's poetry. The *Sunday Times* reviewer, Harold Hobson, accused John of gabbling his lines, and his colleagues all wrote similar criticisms. A black Caribbean actor could not play Shakespeare unless he aped the English of Englishmen. Of course, just a few years later, when Laurence Olivier, at the very same theatre – now the temporary home of the British National Theatre - produced a histrionic caricature of blackness in his Othello, employing almost all the conceivable clichés of black minstrelsy, sucking his lips, rolling his eyes and swinging his gait while blacked out to the nines, it was marked down by the same critics as a triumph of classical character realisation.

Thus parallel struggles were being waged by black actors and playwrights like Errol John and black cricketers like Frank Worrell and their supporters like James, for true respect and a rightful place in their particular worlds of culture. And in their own region too – as powerful cultural interests of the colonial legacy held out to retain their own power against them in the administration of sport, education of the 'Arts' – areas of life and society where imperial attitudes were to last long and strong, well after 'formal' independence was declared in the separate islands. In *Moon on a Rainbow Shawl*, John's forbidden play, Charlie, the veteran black cricketer, remembers how his criticism of such structures 'cause stink' and provoked the end of the line in his inter-island representative career:

CHARLIE: *In them times so when we went Barbados or Jamaica to play cricket they used to treat us like hogs, boy. When we went on tours they put we in any ole kind of boarding house. The best hotels was fer them and the half-scald members of the team. So in Twenty-seven when we was on tour in Jamaica I said either they treat me decent or they send me back. The stink I made got into the newspapers. They didn't send me back. But that was the last intercolony series I ever play. They broke me boy.*

EPHRAIM: *(quietly) For that?*

CHARLIE: *I should of known mey place. If I had known mey place, Eph, I'd a made the team to England the following year. And in them days boy – the English county clubs was out bidding each other fer bowlers like me. But the Big Ones here strangled my future, boy.*[21]

## Lessons of Class

When James writes of his own lower middle class background in Trinidad, and that of his cricketing protagonists like Wilton St. Hill or Learie Constantine, I recognise the class terrain immediately, for it is mine too. No matter I was born thousands of miles and an ocean away in what was still the seat of Empire, the signs and symbols are still the same. Being made as a human being within the same cricket culture, every Saturday and Sunday I looked through the same window, beyond the Essex boundary, onto my father playing cricket. So when James asks me as a reader, 'What do men live by?' I can recognise similar things and the learning process for me was not so different. Cricket and Englishness were woven into me like the thick white sweaters my mother knitted for me almost every new season when I was a boy growing up in the London suburbs in the decade following the war. My parents had met during the hours and rituals of cricket. He would walk around the boundary of Romford cricket ground during his own team's innings. Being an opening bowler and a late-order batsman he had the time to make many a circuit. He often fielded too, on the Third Man boundary. My mother-to-be lived with her elder sister in a house with a garden backing onto the ground, just beyond the boundary. She would look over the fence, he would chat with her. It was the scenario of a suburban idyll made by cricket, and in time produced a cricketing marriage which eventually produced me during 1944, when cricket, like everything else, was rationed – the year of the doodlebugs, when suburban cricket grounds were as vulnerable as anywhere else in London to the potential oblivion of the nazi flying bombs.

Cricket and war were fused for my father. As a strong and talented club cricketer, he had regularly opened the bowling for his club side with the Essex and England fast bowler, Kenneth Farnes, who was to be killed during the war on a practice flight with the R.A.F. In his *Cricket Crisis*[22], Jack Fingleton, the Australian opening batsman, writer and commentator (a figure my father fervently admired, despite his Australianness), wrote of the 'rugged fury' of Farnes' bowling, and described him as 'the most handsome test cricketer of his age, but better than his looks was his modest, cheerful and cultured company.' My father spoke in much the same terms of his opening partner. Like many a cricketer he missed some of his best years through the war and looked back to the two decades before it as an epic era. He had two heroes. One was Douglas Jardine, the captain of the 1932-3 'bodyline' tour of Australia. For my father the 'natural enemy' was never Germany or France. It was Australia, and Jardine and his fastbowling non-commissioned officers, Larwood and Voce, were at the centre of his pantheon. As was the former Essex and England captain, J.W.H.T. ('Johnny Won't Hit Today') Douglas, who exerted a virtually mystical influence over my father's memories of boyhood. He told me that one evening, having missed buying the evening paper, he also missed knowing the overnight Essex score in a county match at Leyton. He found Douglas' phone number in the telephone directory, phoned the Essex captain directly at his home in Wanstead, apologised for his intrusion and asked him the score. Douglas was pleased to tell him: 'Any time you want to know, ring me, son!' he told my father, who never forgot it, and made several other late evening calls on subsequent occasions to the Essex captain. Such were the ways of cricket that stood in his memory.

For my father and many lower middle class men, cricket was a bond of blood. Right through my boyhood, to my late teens as I grew a strong right throwing arm, he would stand ten paces opposite me in the garden, and command me to throw a leather cricket ball directly at his head. He never flinched as I hurled it, and he never dropped a catch. For me, particularly as I grew older and stronger, it was a frightening ritual but seemed an organic part of being a cricketer's son, along with the Saturday and Sunday accompaniment to all home and away matches as team scorer, or the winter evenings – every Monday night – when I was despatched to Romford cricket school in the yard of the Golden Lion public house, with a ten-shilling note in my pocket, for half an hour's coaching from the Essex opening batsman A.V. 'Sonny' Avery.[23] Even now, in my mid-fifties, when I play a correct forward defensive stroke, I remember the mild commands of Avery, who opened the batting for Essex in the decade after the war, scoring 1,000 runs in every successive season.

But cricket for my father was also truly the imperial game and a way of interpreting the world and its cricket-playing peoples. His respect for the enormous cricketing abilities of Bradman, Lindwall or Miller and the generations of Australians was qualified by his doubts about their lack of Britishness and suspect morality. The Indians were definitely untrustworthy – in business they were 'twisters', crafty, liable to cheat, and this also spilled into their cricket – except, the aristocratic ones, the Ranjitsinjis, the Duleepsinjis and Pataudis. The West Indians were flamboyant and often brilliant – he spoke warmly of Learie Constantine whom he saw as the consummate all-rounder, and against whom he had once played and with whom he had shared a drink after the game – a 'real gentleman', he said. But they were flawed, he claimed – they were no good when they were losing, when the pressure was on. They couldn't fight back; they would 'run' like typical colonial troops, before the enemy. For the (white) South Africans and New Zealanders he had an ungrudging admiration: they were truly 'like us', he would declare, and of us too. Thus cricket rendered the imperial 'values' and caricatures perfectly in digestible assertions that were unquestioningly passed on through generations. It took me many years, many experiences and much reflection as well as much passionate and painful argument with my father, to unlearn these things and build a more authentic picture of the people of the post-imperial world. Yet the mediator of that world had undoubtedly been cricket: and cricket was often to break it asunder, as the colonised peoples used the sport of Empire to assert their anti-imperial genius and creativity in those years.

But when James writes about W.G. Grace as an example of a man and cricketer who was 'strong with the strength of men who are filling a social need', so was J.W.H.T. Douglas to my father, for this cricketer represented to him a bonding in the father-son relationship which became exemplary. Douglas' own father was an athlete, boxer and cricket enthusiast who became wealthy as a City-based businessman, owning a firm which imported timber for the construction of staves used in the building trade.24 My father identified strongly with this trade background, working in the Sales Department of a small city commodity broker's firm, a job he had from leaving school at 14 in 1922 until his eventual retirement in the late seventies. Finding buyers and sellers for Chinese bristles comprised his entire professional life, broken up on summer weekends by his love and pursuit of cricket.

The younger Douglas, also a prominent amateur boxer and international footballer, joined his father's firm, which allowed him to play as an amateur for the rest of his cricketing life in a situation of relative privilege. In 1930 however, tragedy struck both father and son. The younger Douglas, as usual, went with his father to Scandinavia during December to purchase timber which would be delivered to Britain when the northern ports unfroze in the Spring. While returning to England in the Finnish ship, the *Oberon*, both father and son were drowned as the vessel went down in thick fog in transit from Helsinki to Hull. My father would tell me how the son lost his life in a last effort to rescue his father, trapped in his cabin, as the ship finally foundered. Of such stories too, his life in cricket was made: sons and fathers, fathers and sons. They became part of a controlling cricket mythology locked into English lower middle class life. For my father too, the cricketing family ideal was that father and son would play together – even open the batting together as we did once in the village ground of his own Essex boyhood. That too was a statement of culture, of cricket life, an essential part of what James analysed, for me too, as 'the framework of my existence', interpreting a set of 'unstated assumptions that are the well springs' of his (and my) thought.[25]

It was a part of the class to which I was acculturated through cricket, as I was to realise only when I first read *Beyond a Boundary* in my twenties, from the Caribbean island where I first became a schoolteacher – a part of James' nation. The book put into lucid perspective my own education as an Englishman and a cricketer – from the books I read as a boy, the public school 'Greyfriars' novels imbued with the cricket culture, with Billy Bunter and the colonial Indian prince – 'Hurree Jamset Ram Singh' and the 'boys' own' story whose title I can never remember, about another cricket-playing maharajah's son at an English public school, who is pursued by a gang of murderous low-class dacoits for his father's precious stone which he carries. His father had forced him into cricket as a right-handed batsman when he was a natural left-hander. It is only towards the end of the novel that the son frees himself from his father's domination, bats left-handed and scores a vital century to enable his school to win a key game over a rival team. The dacoits are captured, the jewel recovered and the father pacified by his son's cricketing success, albeit as a left-hander – as well as realising the errors of his own parenting. This and a thousand other tales in boys' books, comics and cricketing biographies sat within the motto, the moral code burnt into a block of balsa wood, that my father gave me for my bedroom wall, whereby the ethics of a cricket culture took on a quasi-divine dimension:

> *For when the one great scorer comes*
> *To write against your name,*
> *He writes not how you won or lost*
> *But how you played the game.*

'What do men live by?' asks James. This was it.

Yet, as I was to discover – partly through my readings of James - applied to real life, it was a morality surface deep. As I grew into cricket, progressing from school to district to junior county and England sides, I saw how the elements of class and class preference dominated the culture of English representative cricket, from selection to coaching to resources to official encouragement. When James writes of the gradation of cricket according to class and complexion in his boyhood Trinidad, it seemed not so different in England. The issue of race and resources for young black working class cricketers from the inner cities has now also become a major factor in the sport – still being largely ignored in many powerful quarters of the cricket establishment.[26] But during my own boyhood the distinctions were often more subtly revealed, as they were in James' Trinidad. Not by race, but certainly by class, often class within class. When I began to play regularly in Essex junior cricket, the major opportunity was the chance to play for the 'Essex Young Amateurs' team. This was chosen preferentially not only by factors of talent, but more so by school. It was the territory mainly of the public schools – not the most prestigious like Eton, Harrow or Winchester who had their other more powerful cricketing outlets, but lesser-known and minor public schools like Tonbridge, Felsted, Brentwood or Newport. I was a secondary moderner by origin who had made a late entry to a new suburban grammar school which had no cricketing tradition – thus I was very soon and very effectively marginalized by the aspiring public school ethos of the majority of the young players. I discovered that my own lower middle class credentials failed to suffice, and although I enjoyed the cricket – played often at county grounds, sometimes against the skilled young professionals of county Club and Ground sides, I found myself swiftly educated into the subtle violence of a class society, and its sharp gradations. James had written in *Beyond a Boundary* long before I read and understood the words: 'Cricket had plunged me into politics long before I was aware of it.'[27] I discovered them too, suddenly and acutely, when I played for Essex Young Amateurs against the Essex Club and Ground – a virtual 'Gentlemen versus Players' contest. The majority of young working class professionals of the latter, (including two future international players – the leg-spinner Robin Hobbs and Essex and England captain and manager to be, Keith Fletcher) seemed socially intimidated by the confidence, sometimes arrogance, and style of the 'Young Amateurs', and were clearly expected to show a certain respect for their 'betters'. In the event, their batting collapsed, giving even me some cheap wickets and bolstering the overweening assuredness of the public school clique. It was a clear encounter of class played out on a cricket pitch, and an early lesson for me in the way in which English society was graded and fundamentally operated. When I read *Beyond a Boundary* years later in the Caribbean, these Essex moments, astonishingly, like a sudden yorker from the past, came directly back to uproot me.

## San Fernando Rendezvous

I spent my entire boyhood obsessed by cricket – as a typical Essex seambowler, playing and watching. These were the years when England lost its imperial hegemony to the U.S.A., shed its struggling colonies and began to fail abidingly in its cricket. The year of its greatest Ashes dominance, 1956, when the England team, captained by May and symbolised by the unplayable off breaks of Jim Laker and his 19 wickets in one test at Old Trafford, was quickly followed by Nasser reclaiming the Suez Canal for Egypt and the decisive lakering of British imperialism. I was schooled and played on the green Essex wickets through Sharpeville, the D'Oliveira affair and the eventual international isolation of South African cricket, while the mighty West Indian tradition rose to supremacy under the leadership and black captaincy of Worrell and Sobers and the genius on the field of other masters like Kanhai, Gibbs and Hall. I had no idea that such changes had been provoked by the campaigning by James and others for a signal watershed in Caribbean cricket leadership, as the popular struggles and anticolonial leadership of Eric Williams, Cheddi Jagan and Norman Manley had secured formal independence for Trinidad, Guyana and Jamaica. It was only when I read *Beyond a Boundary*, having worked as a teacher in James' own country in the late sixties, that a realisation broke inside me, that to play and read cricket was to read and act in life.

In acknowledgement, and thanking James for the world of living insight that his book has offered me, I shall return to 1982, a few months before I was to finally meet and interview him. While working as a teacher educator in Grenada, I was charged by the People's Revolutionary Government to help establish a publishing initiative. Later called *Fedon Publishers* after the Grenadian who led the 1795 anti-colonial rebellion, it published a number of books narrating various aspects of the progress of Grenada's Revolution. We were invited to visit Trinidad in June 1982 as part of a Grenada delegation to the yearly celebrations at Fyzabad organised by Trinidad and Tobago's Oil Workers Trade Union to commemorate 'Butler Day', when the life and struggle at the migrant Grenadian trade union leader Tubal Uriah

'Buzz' Butler and in particular his part in the 1937 Oil Workers' struggle, was remembered. We were very hospitably invited to sleep at the OWTU headquarters in the southern town of San Fernando during the night before the event.[28]

At suppertime I needed to make a telephone call, and was directed to a room up the corridor from where we were sleeping, which, I was told, had a phone. As soon as I entered the room I could sense it was lived in by someone with a particular personality and strong interests. One bookcase contained the complete works of Marx and Lenin, and many other political works. The other supported what seemed to be a complete set of Wisden Cricket almanacs. On a hook on the inside of the door was a wide-rimmed hat and cape. Who else could be living in this room? Yet what suddenly rendered me breathless was the book, open on the desk of the room's resident, covered with jottings, its pages heavily annotated with margin commentary. It was a book I had written three years before, *We're Building the New School!*[29] about the democratic changes in the education system in Mozambique, from where I had returned in 1980 after a period of teaching in a secondary school. I froze. Without knowing, I had met the writer I most admired. All the way from the London suburbs and the green Essex wickets, and we had met in words of print about revolutionary Africa in a trade union building in the south of Trinidad. I could only marvel. I made my call, nervously, and returned and asked, 'Whose room was that?' 'Mr. James',' said one of the OWTU officials, 'he stays here when he is in Trinidad. At the moment he is away – in England, I believe.'

At least I had the chance to meet him and thank him for his writing and his lifetime's work – for cricket too, and for much more than cricket. I have probably read *Beyond a Boundary* as an adult as many times as James tells that he read *Vanity Fair* as a boy, and it is possible that it has had as similar a huge and lasting impact upon my life, as Thackeray's book had on James'. For with his 'marvellous West Indian brains' that he attributed to Learie Constantine, he had in his own life, in his activism and his writing, achieved what he claimed W.G. Grace had created in his own era: 'He had extended our conception of human capacity' in a culture which he had appropriated, emulated and forged again in the image of his own and all people.

**REFERENCES**

1 See Chapter 2: 'Cricket and the Mirror of Racism'

2 Viv Richards, *Hitting Across the Line* (London, 1993)

3 Ibid.

4 Learie Constantine, *Cricketers' Cricket* (London, 1991)

5 Chris Searle (ed.), *In Nobody's Backyard: Maurice Bishop's Speeches, 1979-1983* (London, 1984)

6 Viv Richards, *Hitting Across the Line*

7 Viv Richards, *Cricket Masterclass* (London, 1988)

8 Learie Constantine, *Cricketers' Cricket*

9 C.L.R. James, *Beyond a Boudary* (Hutchinson, 1969)

10 Ibid.

11 Ibid. See also Wes Hall, *Pace Like Fire* (Pelham Books, 1965)

12 See *Hit Racism for Six: Race and Cricket in England Today* (Centre for Sports Development, Roehampton Institute, London, 1996)

13 Chris Searle, 'Running a gauntlet of hate at Headingley', *Observer* (18 August 1996)

14 Interview published in *Words Unchained: Language and Revolution in Grenada* (London, 1984)

15 C.L.R. James, *Beyond a Boudary*

16 Ibid.

17 Ibid.

18 Errol John, *Moon on a Rainbow Shawl* (London, 1958)

19 The Old Vic Theatre, Programme notes to *Othello* (first performed 30 January 1963, London)

20 See Chris Searle, *The Forsaken Lover, White Words and Black People* (London, 1972, 1973)

21 Errol John, *Moon on a Rainbow Shawl*

22 Jack Fingleton, *Cricket Crisi*

23 See Roy Webber, *Who's Who in World Cricket* (London, 1952)

24 David Lemmon, *Johnny Won't Hit Today: A Cricketing Biography of J. W.H.T Douglas* (London, 1983)

25 C.L.R. James, *Beyond a Boudary*

26 See Chapter Four: 'Towards a Cricket of the Future'

27 C.L.R. James, *Beyond a Boudary*

28 See Chris Searle, *Grenada Morning: a memoir of the 'Revo'* (London, 1989)

29 Chris Searle, *'We're Building the New School!' Diary of a Teacher in Mozambique* (London, 1980)

# 12.

# TALL MEN, AND LIONS TOO

AS AN ENGLISHMAN, I HAVE ALWAYS felt uneasy about the sporting heraldry of three lions on the cricket caps or football shirts of players representing England. It is a historical deception and illusion. These are stolen and appropriated symbols. Lions belong to Africa and Africans and those whom the diaspora has scattered throughout the world. The lion is only found in England in cages, not free and unbound. The lion as a heraldic emblem was the device of English kings – it never belonged to the common man and woman.

So who are the real lions of sport? We have been watching them all through the summer, and two of their names are Walsh and Ambrose, lions and men with what C.L.R. James called 'our great West Indian brains'.

Rare and accomplished cricketers that we have been lucky and privileged to see. But more too. All through their cricketing lives they carry West Indian unity and the promise of a Caribbean nation. Curtly Ambrose from the small eastern Caribbean island of Antigua; Courtney Walsh from the much larger polity of Jamaica: they are patriots of a nation still to be born.

The West Indian nation exists only in a small number of regional institutions, chiefly its university and its cricket team. So to talk of 'patriotism' in the West Indies sense is not reactionary or chauvinistic: it is to speak of a common hope and aspiration, the fulfilment of a dream of a people whose history tells both of the most terrible brutality and betrayal, but of resistance and rebellion too, in politics, in culture, in sport.

When Maurice Bishop made his call, 'One Caribbean!'; when another Grenadian, T.A. Marryshow, set down his dream of Caribbean unity; when the Trinidadian James saw crowds at a West Indies home test as a microcosm of that one entity from Belize to Guyana and all the islands between, their words were as Walsh and Ambrose's bowling. Just as the lyrics and notes of the Jamaican Bob Marley, the poems and metaphors of the St. Lucian Derek Walcott, the novels of the Barbadian George Lamming, the calypso wit of the Trinidadian Sparrow, the jazz trumpet beauty of the Vincentian Shake Keane, the power of dialect and humour of the balladeer Louise Bennett, the spectacular goals of Tobago's Dwight Yorke, the oratory of Fidel Castro, the human example of Che Chevara. They all tell of the Caribbean nation in formation.

With Curtly it is his astonishing consistency. Delivery after delivery, over after over – the accuracy of line and length, the unending travelling along the off-stump pathway, the quality of bounce after the knees-up approach, huge striding and towering release, of deviation off the pitch, the waiting clutches of the slips, the ball relentlessly coming at you, never leaving you, forcing you to play, to risk, to snick, to finish with you, maiden after maiden.

With Courtney, it is all that too but also the wit and hilarity of outrageous variation. Here is a fast bowler as full of tricks as Anansi himself. The slower ball that falls at the batsman's crease or to his toe as it did twice to the bemused Graham Thorpe at Old Trafford and the Oval; the vicious high-speed cutting off break that severs the batsman and takes his stumps or his perplexed legs. The ball which comes in with the air and goes away off the ground, pursuing the bat-edge as if within its leather casing it has a discrete intelligence of its own.

What skill, what brainpower lives within this bowling, and what beauty and nobility of action too, as their onlookers watch and marvel. Walsh's 485, Ambrose's 403 – nearly 900 test match batsmen have fallen to them from all cricketing nations; they have spread cricket devastation wherever they have played. Yet the immense appreciation of them by the London Oval crowd was more than moving: it was more like an act of love. On the last day of this final test in urban September sun they made their exit. With arms around each other and framed by the iron of the giant gasholder, they left the field after the final balls had been delivered. When they came out to bat the next day, one after the other, the England players made a valley of applause for them to pass through. Ambrose answered with some huge swings of the bat, and even with an injured leg, a dancing 28; Walsh seemed almost too moved to lift his bat.

But the tribute in itself was unique, mobilised and led by England's first black captain, the son of another diaspora, from South-East Asia, the east Londoner Nasser Hussain. The huge crowd responded with a hail of clapping. A full Oval, crammed with children let in for free and adults for a tenner, occupying elitist private boxes and unclaimed sponsors' seats and echoed by another five thousand locked out and surging in the streets outside, realised the dignity and achievement of these men, these Caribbean lions.

Earlier in the day, part of an admiring group of watchers of all ages, I queued for Walsh's autograph to give to my son. He duly obliged with warmth and modesty. My mind went racing back to 1957, when as a nervous suburban schoolboy with a passion for cricket and pretensions as a paceman, I approached the Barbadian fast bowler Wes Hall and asked for the same at Ilford, where the West Indies were playing my home county, Essex. I had never spoken to a black man before. The Essex suburbs were lilywhite. It was before Hall's glory years and he had yet to play in a test match. He was young and nervous too, and his friendliness and a certain pride of being made a big impression on me. Over four decades separated these two signings, these miniscule personal events, yet what a burgeoning of a Caribbean people and their living culture did they enfold. The revolutions of Cuba and Grenada, one still thriving, the other imploded and crushed and yet still the image of Bishop in my ears proclaiming to thousands of his Caribbean compatriots, 'We'll hit imperialism for six!'

And cricket central to it all, emblematising a culture; Viv Richards' incredible batting power, the beauty, pace and intelligence of Hall, Roberts, Garner, Holding and the sublime Marshall. The glory, elegance and unparalleled versatility of Sobers, the creative fire and inventiveness that was Kanhai, the guile and persistence that was Gibbs, Lloyd's adroit captaincy and mighty strokeplay; Greenidge's cutting ferocity, Lara's grace and power.

It is all held too within the achievement of these two tall, modest and very dexterous men. Cricketers, West Indians and lions too, the both of them – scourge of batsmen, heroes of the pitch of life.

# APPENDIX

## MEAN STREETS FEEL THE PACE OF CHANGE
(Kevin Mitchell in the *Observer*, 21 May 1995)

THERE IS A SPECIAL FEEL ABOUT SHEFFIELD, tucked away in the rough, rolling hills of South Yorkshire. What others say they can't do, they invariably do, stubbornness informed by a history of struggle, steel running through their past in fact and inclination.

It is palpable at the Earl Marshal School in the north of the city. Here in the blighted district of Fir Vale, where mass unemployment and crime give even a sunny day a hard edge, smiling brown faces, sons of the huge immigrant community, draw comfort from the simple pleasure of bat and ball.

The head teacher is Chris Searle, an Essex man and cricket lover who brings a tireless zeal to his work. He is quietly proud of his charges, and proud too of the inspiration behind a rare and exciting venture, the Devon Malcolm Cricket Centre.

It started in 1990 and taps into a rich seam of talent provided by children from Pakistan, India, the Yemen, Somalia and the Caribbean. Malcolm, who grew up just a few streets away, is no absentee landlord of his dreams and pays regular visits to the school as the skills of Searle's boys are nurtured under the tutelage of Steve Taylor, who used to open the bowling with Malcolm in club cricket here.

It is heart-warming on a grand scale and Searle's politics of care drives his enthusiasm. He points to Wincobank Hill, a mount of earth with symbolism entwined in every blade of grass, and tells them that it was here that the Romans found the locals, unmovable for an irritatingly long time, tucked up in their Celtic fort. It was not far from here, either, that the Chartists blossomed. It was here where the city of steel lingered in the old trade longer than many expected in the face of recession. It was here where the miners drew much comfort during their year-long strike.

'This is not just about cricket,' Searle says, 'It is about responding to

*173*

cultural strength in the community. And around here it is a culture of resistance. What these kids can learn through cricket, they can take back into their studies. I'm a great believer in team games and cricket stimulates unity and provides collective solutions to problems. In that regard, Devon, who is a powerful cricketer, probably the fastest bowler in the world, has been exceptional. He is a genuine and committed human being. C.L.R. James said the most important thing about the game is that a cricketer should be returned to the community – Devon exemplifies that. He has never left his roots and is a great example for other cricketers.

'The real strength of British cricket lies in the inner cities, which the game's administrators have never realised. There are players in these cities who can form the nucleus of a world-beating England team, particularly among the arrivant communities, but they are simply not being developed.'

This is a sore point in Yorkshire, of course, where the county has not exactly rushed to the grimier streets in search of this new talent. That attitude is changing, slowly, and the Yorkshire Cricket Academy Minority Cricket Forum, set up a year after the Earl Marshal project, is at least addressing the issue. But there is a way to go.

'Cricket has always been a suburban and village green game,' Searle says. 'But we should now be creating a new version of the game, where there is terrific dynamism. This is the most disadvantaged school in Sheffield. But cricket is a unifying force for these kids, many of whose families come from the same villages in Kashmir and who have a real sense of community.'

Amir Riaz, captain of the centre's under-15 and under-17 teams, was leaving for Leeds after school that afternoon to try out for a team to play against Yorkshire's cricket academy. Cricket for the young opening batsman is more than a game. 'It is something that keeps kids out of the cafes and smoking drugs,' he says, with a sense of social awareness not that common in the nineties. It is also joy. There are not many spare moments when the boys aren't crashing about all over the place with bats and pads, setting up impromptu games or toiling away in the nets.

And, while Amir is right about cricket occupying time that might otherwise be spent in any manner of devilment, these boys have a genuine thirst for the game. They are good listeners and quick learners, willing to take on board the experience of their mentor Steve Taylor, who has played semi-professional cricket at a demanding level. But they are not automatons. Their shot-making is full of wristy risk, their bowling inventive and they field with spark.

Taylor sees their development with a clinical, admiring eye, 'We've got one young leg-spinner,' he says, 'Nazim Younis, who is 13 or so and plays with the men's first team on Sunday. I would put him in Shane Warne's class. He is phenomenal, turns the ball a foot.'

Taylor is a realist too. He is impatient with Yorkshire County Cricket Club, suspicious that there are many still in place there who want no part of the young Asian talent under their old noses. 'It's not happening fast enough at all,' he says. 'In cricket, especially at Yorkshire, they want everything to be perfect, everything has to be done their perfect way. Even if Devon had been allowed to play for them, they would never have picked him. They take players and then turn them into what they think the perfect player should be.'

He is sad that more Caribbean youngsters do not embrace the game in Yorkshire. 'In a way, it is because their parents don't want the kids to play sport, because they don't want black youth to be stereotyped. Also there is religion; they go to Sunday school in the morning and church in the afternoon. Those that do play sport usually want to play football. They see it on the television – it is on for so many months of the year anyway – and they like the image, especially now that there are so many black players.'

While cricket in this country dithers about giving youth its head and remains seemingly indifferent to the army of inner-city talent, South Africa has launched a townships programme that will recruit up to a million young black cricketers within five years.

It is a damning judgment on the game that the Devon Malcolm Cricket Centre is one of only two of its kind in the entire country. The London Cricket College, which has produced 14 county players in 11 years, is struggling for funds – at a time when £60 million is flowing into the game. Alan Smith, the chief executive of the Test and County Cricket Board, says grass-roots cricket will 'benefit considerably' from this new money. If he went to Sheffield, he would benefit considerably from the counsel of Majid Malik, one of the gaggle of wide-eyed enthusiasts milling around Mr. Searle and Mr. Taylor last week. Asked what cricket means to him, Majid says quietly, 'Pride.'